Consultants
Dr. Kho Tek Hong
Dr. Lee Ngan Hoe

U.S. Consultant
Susan F. Resnick

Author
Dr. Koay Phong Lee

PRIMARY MATHEMATICS
Student Book

Grade 3A

Marshall Cavendish
Education

© 2022 Marshall Cavendish Education Pte Ltd

Published by Marshall Cavendish Education
Times Centre, 1 New Industrial Road, Singapore 536196
Customer Service Hotline: (65) 6213 9688
US Office Tel: (1-914) 332 8888 | Fax: (1-914) 332 1082
E-mail: cs@mceducation.com
Website: www.mceducation.com

First published 2022
Reprinted 2022

ISBN 978-981-49-1140-5

Printed in Singapore

Preface

WELCOME!

The new **PRIMARY MATHEMATICS** program takes you on an exciting and rewarding learning journey. Experience the fun side of math in both the classroom and daily life! Gain new knowledge, share your thinking, and become a confident problem solver of the future!

Each chapter in this book contains these main features.

Chapter Opener contains a picture that shows how math is all around you. Look at the picture and talk about how useful math is in daily life!

Task links what you know to what you will learn. Explore it using objects or pictures and discuss creative ways to solve it with classmates!

Learn teaches you how to solve the Task confidently and helps to equip you with skills to take on challenging math later!

Activity! inspires you to make new discoveries by sharing ideas or playing a game with your classmates. Have fun!

Learn Together helps you gain deeper understanding of the math taught. Learn with your classmates. Your teacher will support you!

Practice On Your Own lets you work on a variety of problems by yourself. See how much you have learned!

Other features in this book:

Recall
helps you to think back on what you have learned, to help you with the new math.

Chapter Practice
provides questions for you to practice applying math concepts.

Performance Task
encourages you to use your skills and knowledge to try to solve real-world problems! Reflect on your learning through a checklist.

Solve! Heuristics
guides you to use a variety of strategies to solve problems confidently!

 ## Math Talk
invites you to use mathematical language to share your thinking with classmates.

Think!
challenges you to come up with new ideas or ways to solve problems.

 ## STEAM
encourages you to be creative! Use what you have learned in Math and work on a group project that involves Science, Technology, Engineering, or Arts.

Are you ready to begin this exciting learning journey? Let's go!

Contents

Solve! Heuristics: Look for a Pattern

Chapter

4

MULTIPLICATION AND DIVISION OF 6, 7, 8, AND 9

Solve! Heuristics: Guess and Check

Chapter

5

TIME

Glossary

Index

1 NUMBERS TO 10,000

At a state fair, Ellie can exchange game tickets for one prize.

Prize Exchange

3,200 tickets

5,000 tickets

700 tickets

1,600 tickets

Which prize can Ellie get with 3,500 tickets?

Recall

1. Count and write the numbers.

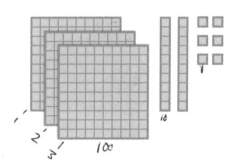

326

2. Write the numbers in standard form.

(a) four hundred seventeen 417

(b) nine hundred five 905

17

3. Write the numbers in word form.

(a) 845 _eight hundred forty five_

(b) 720 _Seven hundred twonee_

4. Write the missing numbers.

(a) 4 hundreds 8 tens 5 ones = _485_

(b) 813 = _813_ hundreds 1 ten 3 ones

5. Write the numbers in expanded form.

(a) 187 = _100_ + _80_ + _70_

(b) 940 = _900_ + _40_ + _00_

6. Write the missing numbers.

(a) __550__ is 1 more than 549.

(b) __770__ is 10 less than 780.

(c) __5100__ is 10 more than 490. +10

(d) 345 is __100__ more than 245.

7. Fill in the missing numbers in the number patterns.

(a) 32, 34, 36, 38, 40, __42__ , __44__

(b) 87, 84, 81, __78__ , __75__ , 72, 69

8. Write <, =, or >.

(a) 450 ⬭ 499

(b) 178 ⬭ 187

(c) 814 ⬭ 481

(d) 670 ⬭ 600 + 70

9. Which group shows the numbers in order from greatest to least?

Ⓐ 708, 780, 807, 870

Ⓑ 780, 870, 708, 807

Ⓒ 807, 870, 708, 780

Ⓓ 870, 807, 780, 708

10. Write the missing numbers.

435 __436__ __438__ 439 __450__ __441__ 445

II. Draw arrows to show the positions of the numbers on the
number lines.

(a) 578

(b) 837

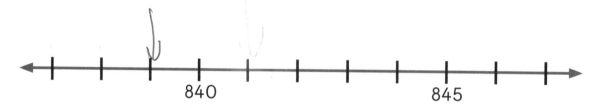

I can...

☐ count and write numbers within 1,000.

☐ write numbers within 1,000 in standard form, word form, and
expanded form.

☐ count on and count back by 1s, 10s, or 100s.

☐ identify patterns and find missing numbers in the patterns.

☐ compare numbers within 1,000 using >, =, or <.

☐ compare and order numbers within 1,000.

☐ find the missing number within 1,000 given its position on a number line.

☐ find the position of a given number within 1,000 on a number line.

1A Place Value

Learn

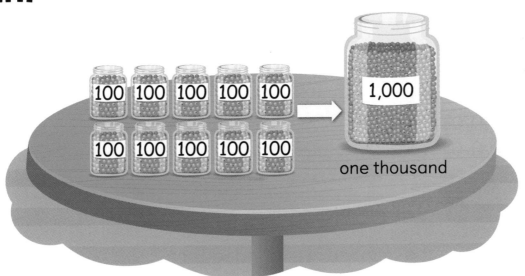

one thousand

___10___ hundreds = 1 thousand
                  = 1,000

___2___ thousands = 2,000

Learn Together

1. Count.

    (a)

    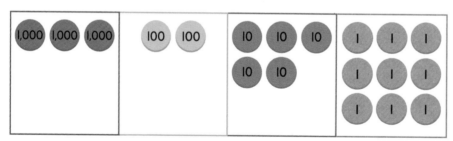

    1,000 1,000 1,000 1,000 1,000

    1,000 1,000 1,000 1,000 1,000

    1,000, 2,000, 3,000, ...,
    9,000, 10,000

    10,000

    ten thousand

    10 thousands = _10+1000_

    (b)

    100 100 100 10 10 10 1 1 1

    100 100 10 10 10 1

    564

    (c)

    1,000 1,000 1,000 100 100 100 10 1 1

    1,000 1,000 1,000

    6312

2.

    1,000 1,000 1,000   100 100   10 10 10   1 1 1

                                      10 10   1 1 1

                                                   1 1 1

    3 0 0 0
      2 0 0
        5 0
         9   ➡   3 2 5 9

    (a) Write the number in expanded form.

    3,259 = 3,000 + 200 + _50_ + _p_

    (b) Write the number in word form.

    three thousands two hundreds

    fiftynine

3.

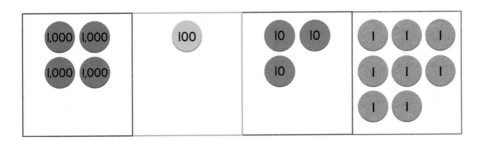

Thousands	Hundreds	Tens	Ones
4	1	3	8

In 4,138,

(a) the digit 4 is in the ___Thousands___ place.

It stands for __4000__.

(b) the value of the digit 1 is __100__.

(c) the digit 3 stands for __30__.

(d) the digit __8__ is in the ones place.

4. I am a 4-digit number.
The digit 4 is in the ones place.
The digit 9 is in the tens place.
The digit 7 is in the hundreds place.
The digit 1 is in the thousands place.

Thousands	Hundreds	Tens	Ones
1	7	9	4

What number am I? __1794__

5. Write the numbers in expanded form.

    (a) 1,628 = 1,000 + <u>600</u> + 20 + 8

    (b) 5,017 = <u>5000</u> + 10 + 7

    (c) 8,009 = <u>800</u> + 9

Activity!

USE TOOLS AND MODEL Use  to represent **two thousand, four hundred seven**. Draw a picture to show the number. Write the number in standard form.

> Explain how you write the number in expanded form.

Practice On Your Own

I. Write the missing numbers.

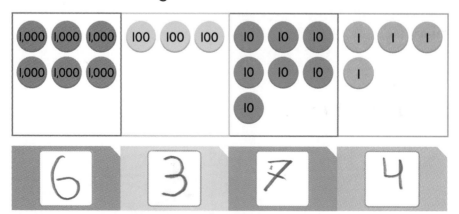

Name: _____ Date: _____

2. What numbers are shown below?

(a)

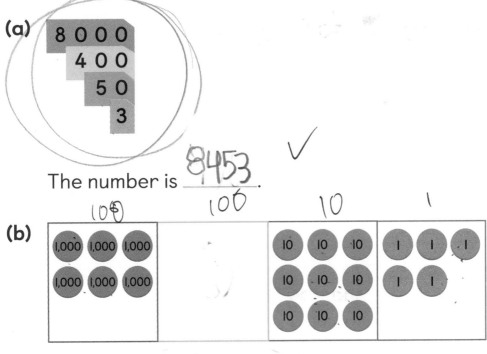

```
8 0 0 0
  4 0 0
    5 0
      3
```

The number is _8453_ ✓

(b)

(100) 100 10 1

The number is _6,097_.

3. I am a 4-digit number.
The digit 5 is in the thousands place.
The digit 2 is in the hundreds place.
The digit 4 is in the tens place.
The digit 8 is in the ones place.

Thousands	Hundreds	Tens	Ones
5	2	4	8

✓

What number am I? _5248_

4. Write nine thousand, two hundred three in standard form.

P23

5. Write 7,410 in word form.

Sivin for ten

6. Write the numbers in standard form.

(a) $2,000 + 200 + 30 + 6 =$ _2236_

(b) $9,000 + 500 + 40 =$ _954_

7. Write the numbers in expanded form.

(a) $4,017 = 4,000 +$ _7236_ $+$ _8861_

(b) $6,921 =$ _6812_ $+ 900 +$ _800_ $+$ _700_

8. In 3,794,

(a) the digit _3_ is in the thousands place.

Its value is _3000_.

(b) The value of the digit 7 is _300_.

(c) The digit 9 stands for _90_.

(d) The digit _4_ is in the ones place.

Think!

9. REASON Is $7,000 + 100 + 39$ the expanded form of 7,139? Explain your answer.

1B Compare and Order Numbers

Richmond
7,702

Little Compton
3,484

The population of Richmond in Rhode Island is 7,702.
The population of Little Compton in Rhode Island is 3,484.
Which town has a larger population?

Learn

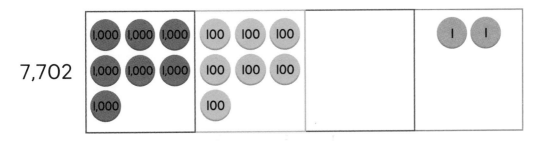

7,702

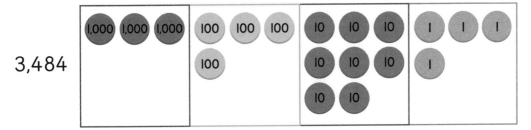

3,484

7,702 > 3,484

7 thousands are greater than 3 thousands.

Richmond has a larger population.

Learn Together

1. Which is greater, 6,312 or 5,743?

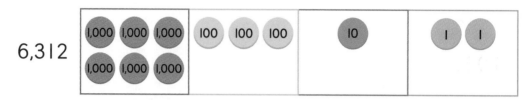

6,312

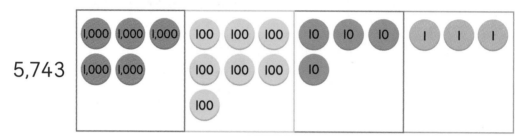

5,743

__6312__ is greater than __5743__.

6312 > 5743

Compare the thousands.

2. Which is less, 5,189 or 5,201?

	Thousands	Hundreds	Tens	Ones
5,189	5	1	8	9
5,201	5	2	0	1

There are 5 thousands in both numbers. Compare the hundreds.

__5189__ is less than __5201__.

5189 < 5201

3. **(a)** Which number is the greatest?

	Thousands	Hundreds	Tens	Ones
4,276	4	2	7	6
5,068	5	0	6	8
4,195	4	1	9	5

_5068_ is the greatest.

5 thousands are greater than 4 thousands.

(b) Which is greater, 4,276 or 4,195?

_4276_ is greater than _4195_.

When the thousands are the same, compare the hundreds.

(c) Order the numbers from greatest to least.

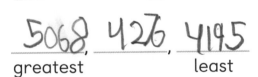
4,276 ✓   5,068 ✓   4,195

_5068_, _426_, _4195_
greatest   least

 What can you say about ordering three numbers?

Practice On Your Own

1. Which is less, 3,587 or 3,609?

	Thousands	Hundreds	Tens	Ones
3,587	3	5	8	7
3,609	3	6	0	9

_3609_ is less than _3587_.

2. Write <, =, or >.

(a) 4,206 $>$ 4,026 ✗

(b) 9,005 $<$ 9,050 ✓

(c) 5,843 $=$ 5,000 + 800 + 40 + 3 ✓

3. (a) Fill in the place-value chart.

	Thousands	Hundreds	Tens	Ones
6,945	6000	900	40	5
7,852	7000	800	50	2
7,389	7000	300	80	9

(b) Order the numbers from least to greatest.

6945 7389 7852

least   greatest

4. Order the numbers from greatest to least.

3,008	3,800	4,018

4018, 3800, 3008   ✓

greatest   least

5. REASON What is the least 4-digit number that you can make using the digits 4, 6, I, and 5? Explain your answer.

1C Number Patterns

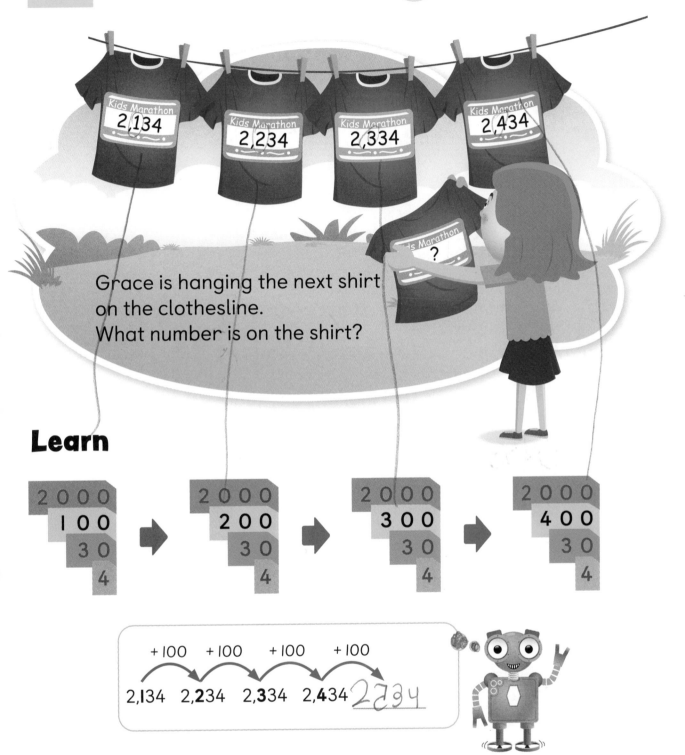

Grace is hanging the next shirt on the clothesline.
What number is on the shirt?

Learn

The numbers make a pattern.
Each number is **100 more** than the number before it.

The number on the shirt is _2734_

Learn Together

1. **(a)** What number is **1,000 more** than 4,851?

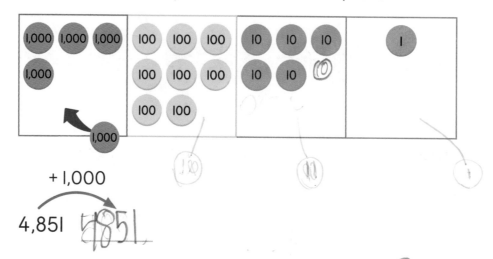

$+ 1,000$

4,851   4851

(b) What number is **1 more** than 4,851? 4852

(c) What number is **10 more** than 4,851? 4861

(d) What number is **100 more** than 4,851? 4951

2. **(a)** What number is **1,000 less** than 6,729?

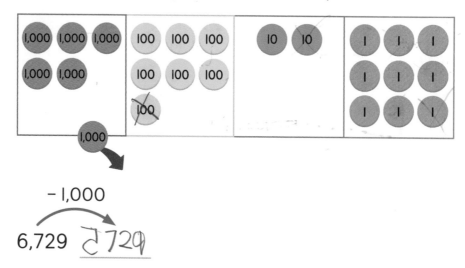

$- 1,000$

6,729   5729

(b) What number is **1 less** than 6,729? 6728

(c) What number is **10 less** than 6,729? 6719

(d) What number is **100 less** than 6,729? 6629

3.

Write the missing number in the number pattern.

$-1,000$ $-1,000$ $-1,000$

9,241, 8,241, 7,241, <u>6241</u>

Activity!

USE TOOLS AND MODEL Use  to show 3,487.
What is 1 more than <u>3,487</u>? How would you find the answer?
Repeat to find 10 more, 100 more, and 1,000 more than 3,487.

Practice On Your Own

1. **(a)** Fill in the place-value chart.

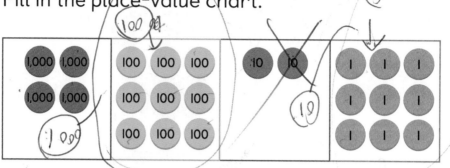

Thousands	Hundreds	Tens	Ones
4006	900	2	10

(b) 3929 is 1,000 less than 4,929.

(c) 4929 is 10 less than 4,929.

(d) 4930 is 1 more than 4,929.

(e) 5029 is 100 more than 4,929.

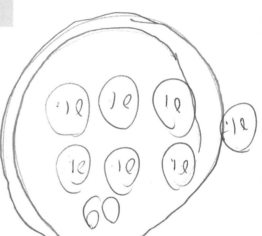

2. Fill in the missing numbers in the number patterns.

(a) 1,367, 1,377, 1,387, 1,397, 1407, 2227

(b) 5,421, 5,321, 5,221, 5,121, 5021, 4921

(c) 9803, 8,803, 7,803, 6,803, 5,803, 4803

3. Fill in the blanks.

| 3,615 | 3,616 | 3,617 | ? | 3,619 | ? |

(a) Each number is __1 more__ than the number before it.

(b) The number which comes just after 3,617 in the pattern is
   _3618_

(c) The number which comes just after 3,619 in the pattern is
   _3620_.

4. REASON Show and explain two ways to make a number pattern using these numbers.

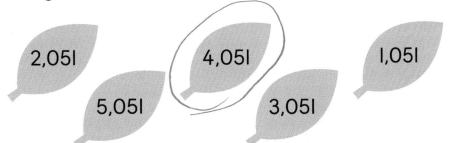

2,051   4,051   1,051
   5,051   3,051

Think!

5. REASON The numbers on the mailboxes in an apartment building make patterns.

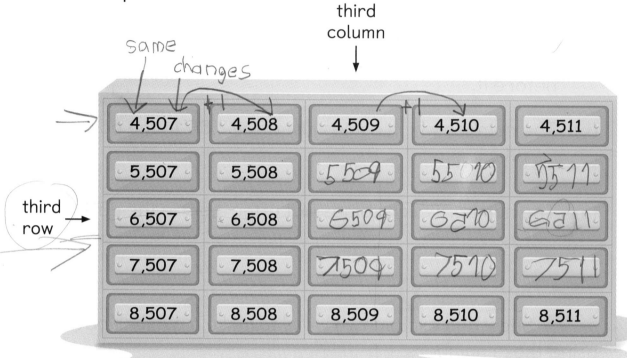

(a) What is the number pattern in the third row of the mailboxes? Explain your answer.

The 1 are go up by 1

(b) What is the number pattern in the third column of the mailboxes? Explain your answer.

The 1000 is change

1D Rounding Numbers

Lucia, Ethan, and Ali each bought a book from the bookstore.

Book A $38

Book B $25

Book C $22

I paid about $20 for my book. (Lucia)

I paid about $40 for my book. (Ethan)

I paid about $30 for my book. (Ali)

Which book did each of the children buy?

Learn

The children **rounded** the cost of the books to the nearest ten dollars.

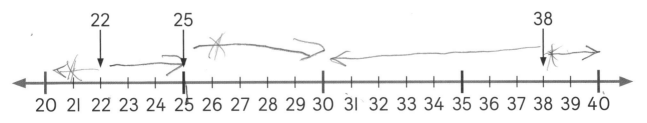

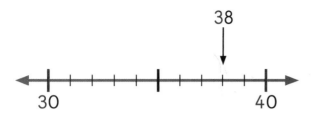

38 is between 30 and 40.
It is nearer to 40 than to 30.

38 is 40 when rounded to the nearest ten.
Ethan bought Book A.

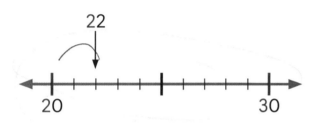

22 is between 20 and 30.
It is nearer to 20 than to 30.

22 is 20 when rounded to the nearest ten.
Lucia bought Book C.

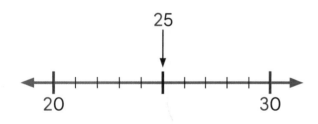

25 is halfway between 20 and 30.
I round up to the nearest ten.

25 is 30 when rounded to the nearest ten.
Ali bought Book B.

Learn Together

I. Round 639 to the nearest hundred.

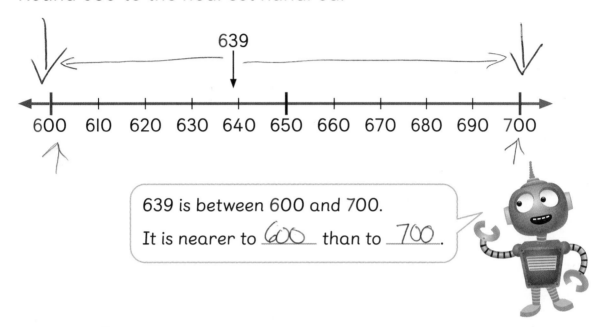

639 is between 600 and 700.

It is nearer to _600_ than to _700_.

639 is _600_ when rounded to the nearest hundred.

2. Round 2,478 to the nearest hundred.

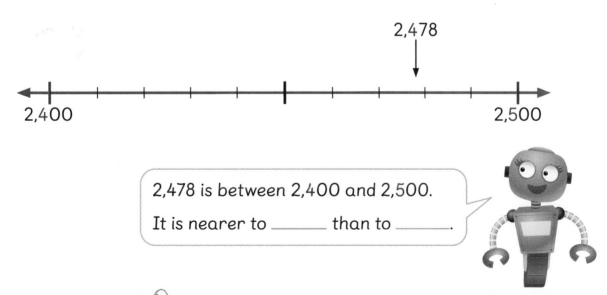

2,478 is between 2,400 and 2,500.

It is nearer to _____ than to _____.

2,478 is _2500_ when rounded to the nearest hundred.

3. Use the number line to round each number to the nearest ten.

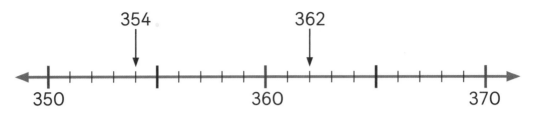

(a) 354 is between 350 and 360.

354 is nearer to 350 than to 360.

354 is _350_ when rounded to the nearest ten.

(b) 362 is between 360 and 370.

362 is nearer to _360_ than to _370_.

362 is _360_ when rounded to the nearest ten.

Practice On Your Own

1. Use the number line to round each number to the nearest hundred.

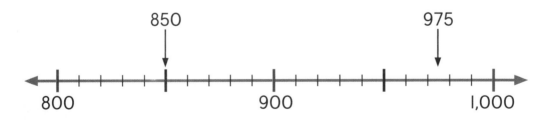

(a) 850 is _900_ when rounded to the nearest hundred.

(b) 975 is _1,000_ when rounded to the nearest hundred.

2. There are 1,684 people at a concert.

(a) Round the number of people to the nearest ten.

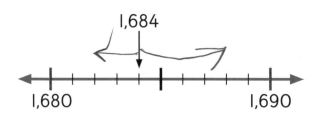

1,684 is __1,690__ when rounded to the nearest ten.

(b) Round the number of people to the nearest hundred.

1,684 is __1,700__ when rounded to the nearest hundred.

3. Round each number to the nearest ten.

(a) 463 _____   **(b)** 645 _____

(c) 1,756 _____   **(d)** 5,407 _____

4. Round each number to the nearest hundred.

(a) 637 _____   **(b)** 394 _____

(c) 8,450 _____   **(d)** 4,870 _____

Think!

5. `REASON` A number is 60 when rounded to the nearest ten. What could the number be? Explain your answer.

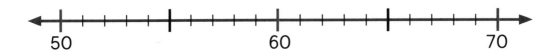

6. `REASON` A number is 500 when rounded to the nearest hundred. What could the greatest possible number be? Explain your answer.

Performance Task

A company ships boxes of goods in containers.
Each blue container can hold up to 1,000 boxes.
Each red container can hold up to 100 boxes.
Each green container can hold up to 10 boxes.
The container has to be fully filled before it can be shipped out.

1. The company ships 7 blue containers, 4 red containers, and
    3 green containers on Monday. How many boxes does the
    company ship in all?

    The company ships _____ boxes in all.

2. The company ships 3 blue containers, 6 red containers, and
    5 green containers on Tuesday. 1 red container is lost during
    the shipping. How many boxes arrive at the destination?

    _____ boxes arrive at the destination.

3. **(a)** The company has to ship 5,920 boxes on Wednesday. Using the fewest number of containers, how many of each colored container does it need?

The company needs _____ blue containers, _____

red containers, and _____ green containers.

(b) MODEL Some boxes are damaged during the shipping. The number of damaged boxes when rounded to the nearest ten is 190. What is the fewest possible number of damaged boxes? Draw a number line to show how you arrive at your answer.

4. MODEL The company ships 10 containers on Friday. There is 1 more red container than blue containers. The number of green containers is the fewest. Use  to show your work and find the total number of boxes.

How Did I Do?

☺☺☺	☐ My work is accurate. ☐ I explain my thinking clearly. ☐ I can apply my thinking in word problems. ☐ I can justify why my strategy fits the situation.
☺☺	☐ I am mostly accurate. ☐ I explain my thinking clearly. ☐ I can apply my thinking to calculations. ☐ I can use multiple strategies.
☺	☐ I show little work. ☐ I do not explain my thinking clearly. ☐ I am struggling with word problems. ☐ I can only think of one way to solve a problem.

My Teacher's Words

 **Project Work**

Tall, taller, tallest

Many of the world's tallest buildings stand out because of the architecture and design. Buildings contain offices, shops, and homes. Which is the tallest building you have ever seen?

Task

1. Use the internet to search for the five tallest buildings in the United States.

2. Find out the science behind the architecture of each building.

3. Record the heights of the buildings in feet using a table.

4. Round the height of each building to the nearest ten feet.

5. Cut out and label strips of paper to represent each building.

6. Compare the heights of the buildings. What is the difference in height between the tallest and shortest buildings?

7. Design a building on another strip of paper. Name your building and write its height.

8. Show where your building will rank among the five tallest buildings you found.

Chapter Practice

1. Which number is 800 when rounded to the nearest hundred?

(A) 850

(B) 748

(C) 794

(D) 865

2. Write the numbers in standard form.

(a) four thousand, five hundred thirteen _____

(b) eight thousand, twenty _____

3. Write the numbers in word form.

(a) 5,326 _____

(b) 9,042 _____

4. Fill in the blanks.

(a) In 3,946, the digit _____ is in the ones place.

(b) In 7,258, the value of 5 is _____.

(c) In 1,029, the digit in the hundreds place is _____.

(d) In 2,681, the digit _____ is in the thousands place.

5. Write the numbers in expanded form.

(a) 5,621 = _____ + _____ + _____ + _____

(b) 2,073 = _____ + _____ + _____ + _____

6. Write the numbers in standard form.

(a) 5,000 + 300 + 60 + 2 = _____

(b) 8,000 + 800 + 80 = _____

(c) _____ = 3 + 40 + 3,000

7. What is the value of the digit 5 in the numbers below?

(a) 6,215 _____   (b) 7,651 _____

(c) 5,093 _____   (d) 1,528 _____

8. Write <, =, or >.

(a) 8,190 ◯ 8,109

(b) 1,305 ◯ 1,000 + 300 + 50

(c) 2,791 ◯ 2,000 + 700 + 90 + 1

9. Order the numbers from greatest to least.

| 5,470 | 4,075 | 4,750 | 5,704 |

_____ , _____ , _____ , _____
greatest   least

10. Fill in the blanks.

(a) _____ is 1,000 more than 3,792.

(b) 4,567 is 100 less than _____.

(c) _____ is 10 more than 3,792.

11. Find the missing numbers in the number patterns.

(a) 3,124, 3,224, 3,324, 3,424, _____

(b) 1,227, 1,217, 1,207, _____, 1,187

(c) 909, 809, 709, 609, _____

12. REASON A number is 240 when rounded to the nearest ten.
(a) Mark **X** on the number line to show the possible numbers.
Explain your answer.

(b) What is the least possible number? _____

13. PERSEVERE Yong, Emilio, and Jayla each pick a 4-digit number.
Emilio's number is 4,580 when rounded to the nearest ten.
Jayla's number is 10 more than Emilio's number.
Yong's number is 100 less than Jayla's number.
Match to show the number each child picks.

4,486

4,586

Yong

4,575

Emilio

4,686

Jayla

4,576

2 ADDITION AND SUBTRACTION WITHIN 10,000

You and Ana played a video game.

Ana's score	SCORE BOARD	Your score
665	ROUND 1	1,645
2,610	ROUND 2	525
1,385	ROUND 3	2,590

Did you win the game? How did you know?

Recall 📝

1. Add or subtract mentally.

   (a) $3 + 9 =$ _____

   (b) $9 + 6 =$ _____

   (c) $16 - 7 =$ _____

   (d) $15 - 9 =$ _____

2. Add. Show your work.

   (a) $365 + 24 =$ _____

   (b) $217 + 712 =$ _____

3. Subtract. Show your work.

   (a) $538 - 26 =$ _____

   (b) $485 - 281 =$ _____

4. Round 467 to the nearest ten. Which is the correct answer?

   (A) 460

   (B) 470

   (C) 400

   (D) 500

5. Which number gives 900 when rounded to the nearest hundred?

   (A) 839

   (B) 845

   (C) 918

   (D) 962

6. Aubrey has 67 game cards.
Her brother gives her another 45 game cards.
How many game cards does Aubrey have in all?

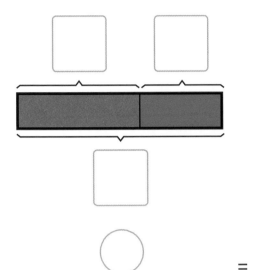

_____ ◯ _____ = _____

Aubrey has _____ game cards in all.

7. Farmer Luke has 306 eggs.
He sells 158 eggs.
How many eggs does Farmer Luke have left?

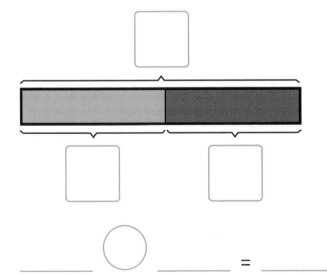

_____ ◯ _____ = _____

Farmer Luke has _____ eggs left.

8. There are 91 adults at a carnival.
   There are 18 fewer children than adults.
   (a) How many children are at the carnival?
   (b) How many adults and children are at the carnival in all?

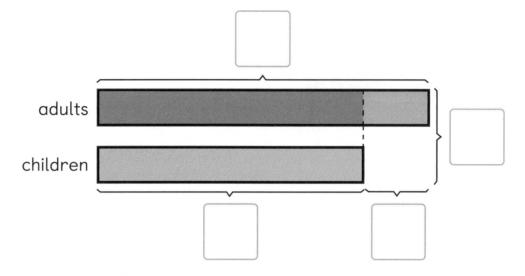

(a) _____ ◯ _____ = _____

_____ children are at the carnival.

(b) _____ ◯ _____ = _____

_____ adults and children are at the carnival in all.

I can...

- ☐ add or subtract within 20 fluently.
- ☐ add a 3-digit and a 2-digit or 3-digit number without renaming within 1,000.
- ☐ subtract a 2-digit or 3-digit number from a 3-digit number without renaming within 1,000.
- ☐ round to the nearest ten or hundred.
- ☐ solve a 1-step word problem involving addition or subtraction within 1,000.
- ☐ solve a 2-part word problem involving addition and subtraction within 1,000.

2A Addition and Subtraction Within 1,000

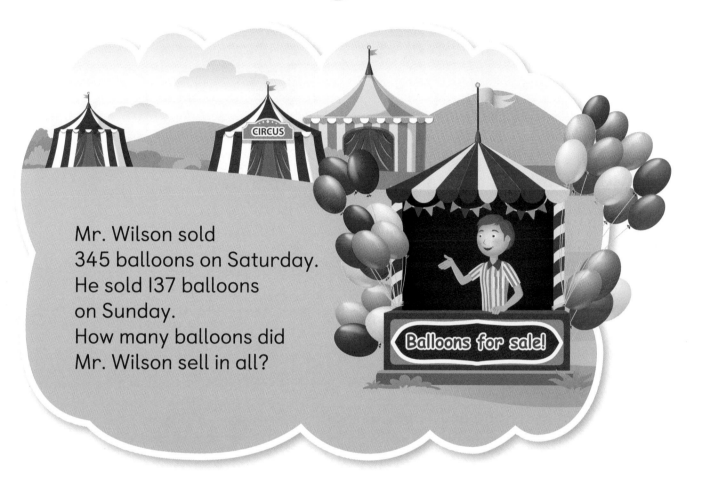

Mr. Wilson sold
345 balloons on Saturday.
He sold 137 balloons
on Sunday.
How many balloons did
Mr. Wilson sell in all?

Balloons for sale!

Learn

Add to find the **sum** of 345 and 137.

Estimate the answer first.
345 is about 350.
137 is about 140.
350 + 140 = 490
The answer is reasonable
if it is close to 490.

345 + 137 = ?

Add the ones.	Add the tens.	Add the hundreds.
H T O 3 4 5 + 1 3 7 ‾‾‾‾‾ 2	H T O 3 4 5 + 1 3 7 ‾‾‾‾‾ 8 2	H T O 3 4 5 + 1 3 7 ‾‾‾‾‾ 4 8 2

There are more than 10 ones.
Rename 10 ones as 1 ten.

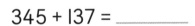

345 + 137 = _____

Mr. Wilson sold _____ balloons in all.

482 is close to 490.
The answer is reasonable.

Learn Together

1. Add. You may use  to help you.

542 + 249 = _____

```
  H T O
    5 4 2
  + 2 4 9
  ───────
```

Rename 10 ones as 1 ten.

2. Add.

654 + 289 = _____

```
    6 5 4
  + 2 8 9
  ───────
```

Rename 10 ones as 1 ten and 10 tens as 1 hundred.

Activity!

Think of two 3-digit numbers. Find the sum of the two numbers. Share how you find your answer with your classmate.

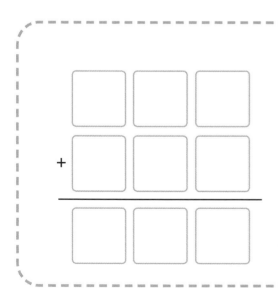

Practice On Your Own

1. Add.

   517 + 483 = _____

2. Find the sum. Show your work.

   (a) 347 + 536 = _____

   (b) 638 + 162 = _____

Farmer Leah picked 555 apples.
She sold 362 apples.
How many apples did she
have left?

Leah's
Apple Farm

Learn

Subtract to find the **difference** between 555 and 362.

Estimate the answer first.
555 is about 560.
362 is about 360.
560 − 360 = 200
The answer is reasonable
if it is close to 200.

555 − 362 = ?

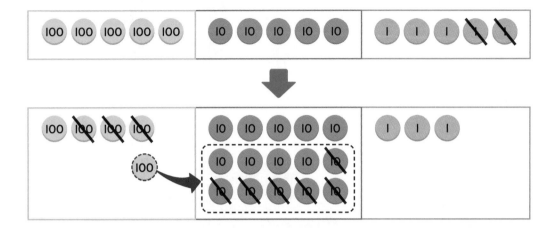

Subtract the ones.	Subtract the tens.	Subtract the hundreds.

Subtract the ones.

```
  H T O
  5 5 5
- 3 6 2
      3
```

Subtract the tens.

```
      4 15
  H T O
  5 5̶ 5
- 3 6 2
    9 3
```

Subtract the hundreds.

```
      4 15
  H T O
  5̶ 5̶ 5
- 3 6 2
  1 9 3
```

There are not enough tens to subtract from.
Rename I hundred as 10 tens.

555 − 362 = _____

She had _____ apples left.

193 is close to 200.
The answer is reasonable.

Learn Together

1. Subtract. You may use 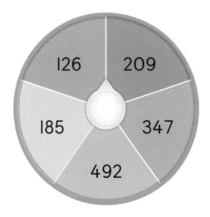 to help you.

   845 – 329 = _____

   ```
    H T O
    8 4 5
   – 3 2 9
   ─────────
   ```

2. Subtract.

   704 – 235 = _____

   ```
    7 0 4
   – 2 3 5
   ─────────
   ```

Activity!

Spin both spinners once to get two numbers.

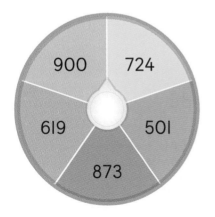

Find the difference between the two numbers.
Color the answer on the next page.

375	434	515	664	553
410	691	9	539	272
377	526	127	774	154
715	688	292	493	598
316	232	408	381	747

Practice On Your Own

1. Subtract.

   613 − 246 = _____

2. Find the difference. Show your work.

   (a) 894 − 438 = _____   **(b)** 800 − 436 = _____

2B Addition and Subtraction Within 10,000

SALE
$1,123

SALE
$1,243

Can you buy both items with $2,000?

Learn

Add to find the total cost.

Estimate the answer first.
1,123 is about 1,100.
1,243 is about 1,200.
1,100 + 1,200 = 2,300
The answer is reasonable
if it is close to 2,300.

1,123 + 1,243 = ?

1,000	100	10 10	1 1 1
1,000	100 100	10 10 10 10	1 1 1

1,000 1,000	100 100 100	10 10 10 10 10 10	1 1 1 1 1 1

1,123 + 1,243 = _____

The total cost is $_____.

2, 366 > 2,000
$2,000 is not enough to buy both items.

2,366 is close to 2,300.
The answer is reasonable.

Activity!

USE TOOLS AND MODEL Use  to show the sum of 2,457 and 1,530.
Draw it out.

Learn Together

1. Add. You may use to help you.

   4,352 + 631 = _____

Th	H	T	O
	4	3	5	2
+		6	3	1

2. Add.

   2,731 + 5,117 = _____

Th	H	T	O
	2	7	3	1
+	5	1	1	7

Practice On Your Own

1. Find the sum. Show your work.

    (a) 8,423 + 564 = _____

    (b) 4,013 + 2,374 = _____

    (c) 9,134 + 712 = _____

    (d) 3,217 + 6,430 = _____

Think!

2. CONSTRUCT VIABLE ARGUMENTS Tyler added 4,318 and 320 in the following way. Do you agree with him? Explain your thinking.

    ```
      4 3 1 8
    + 3 2 0
    ─────────
      7 5 1 8
    ```

Mr. Young went on a vacation.
He spent $1,472 on his plane tickets and
$367 for his stay in a hotel.
How much did Mr. Young
spend in all?

472 + 367 = ?
1,472 + 367 = ?

Learn

Find the sum of $1,472 and $367.

Estimate the answer first.
1,472 is about 1,500.
367 is about 400.
1,500 + 400 = 1,900
The answer is reasonable
if it is close to 1,900.

1,472 + 367 = ?

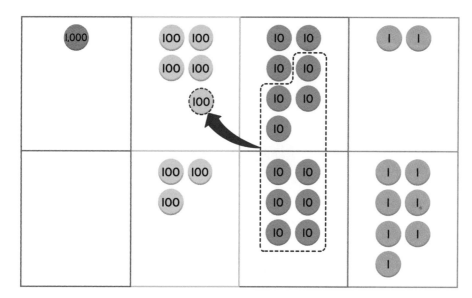

There are more than 10 tens.
Rename 10 tens as 1 hundred.

1,472 + 367 = _____

Mr. Young spent $_____ in all.

1,839 is close to 1,900.
The answer is reasonable.

Add the ones.

Th	H	T	O
1	4	7	2
+		3	6	7
			9

Add the tens.

Th	H	T	O
	1		
1	4	7	2
+		3	6	7
		3	9

Add the hundreds.

Th	H	T	O
	1		
1	4	7	2
+		3	6	7
	8	3	9

Add the thousands.

Th	H	T	O
	1		
1	4	7	2
+		3	6	7
1	8	3	9

Learn Together

Add. You may use 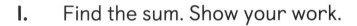 to help you.

I.   1,536 + 2,138 = _____

2.   6,347 + 495 = _____

```
 Th  H  T  O
     1  5  3  6
  +  2  1  3  8
  _____
```

```
 Th  H  T  O
     6  3  4  7
  +     4  9  5
  _____
```

Practice On Your Own

I.   Find the sum. Show your work.

(a) 3,563 + 4,318 = _____   **(b)** 3,874 + 651 = _____

(c) 1,826 + 6,657 = _____   **(d)** 1,896 + 357 = _____

2. Form the greatest and the least 4-digit numbers using the number cards below. Use each number card only once. Then find the sum of the two numbers.

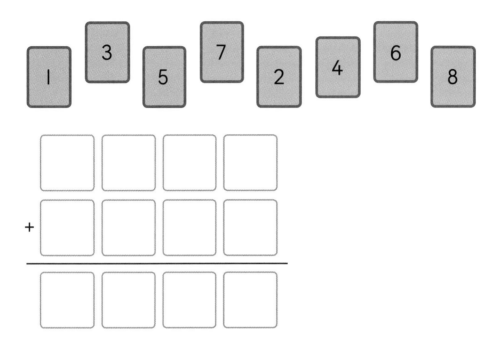

3. CONSTRUCT VIABLE ARGUMENTS Is this addition correct? Show how you can tell without carrying out the addition.

$$
\begin{array}{r}
2\ 0\ 7\ 2 \\
+\ \ \ 8\ 1\ 8 \\
\hline
2\ 8\ 8\ 0
\end{array}
$$

There were 5,673 people at a theme park. It rained and 2,532 people went home. How many people stayed at the theme park?

Learn

Find the difference between 5,673 and 2,532.

Estimate the answer first.
5,673 is about 5,700.
2,532 is about 2,500.
5,700 − 2,500 = 3,200
The answer is reasonable if it is close to 3,200.

5,673 − 2,532 = ?

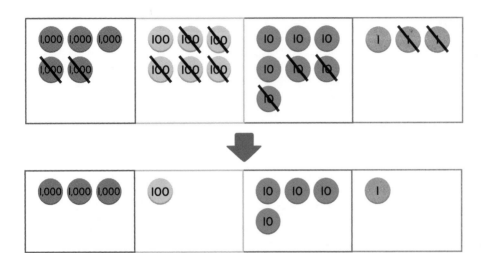

5,673 − 2,532 = _____

_____ people stayed at the theme park.

3,141 is close to 3,200.
The answer is reasonable.

Subtract the ones.

Th	H	T	O
5	6	7	3
− 2	5	3	2
			1

Subtract the tens.

Th	H	T	O
5	6	7	3
− 2	5	3	2
		4	1

Subtract the hundreds.

Th	H	T	O
5	6	7	3
− 2	5	3	2
	☐	4	1

Subtract the thousands.

Th	H	T	O
5	6	7	3
− 2	5	3	2
☐	☐	4	1

Learn Together

1. Subtract. You may use to help you.

7,269 − 137 = _____

Th	H	T	O
7	2	6	9
−	1	3	7

2. 5,647 − 5,123 = _____

Th	H	T	O
5	6	4	7
− 5	1	2	3

3. 2,876 − 1,853 = _____

Th	H	T	O
2	8	7	6
− 1	8	5	3

Practice On Your Own

1. Find the difference. Show your work.

(a) 6,387 − 350 = _____

(b) 8,746 − 221 = _____

(c) $7{,}923 - 6{,}312 =$ _____

(d) $4{,}978 - 1{,}074 =$ _____

Think!

2. USE MATH LANGUAGE Is this subtraction correct? Show two ways you can tell without carrying out the subtraction.

```
   4 8 9 8
 - 1 0 1 3
 ─────────
   3 0 8 5
```

Piano A   **Piano B**

Mr. Collins wants to buy a piano.
Which piano costs more?
How much more? How can you tell?

Learn

Find the difference between $7,263 and $6,321.

Estimate the answer first.
7,263 is about 7,300.
6,321 is about 6,300.
7,300 − 6,300 = 1,000
The answer is reasonable
if it is close to 1,000.

7,263 − 6,321 = ?

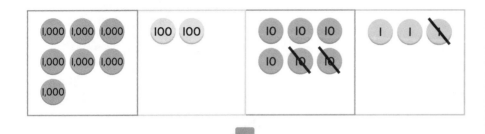

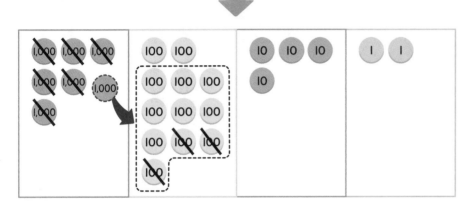

There are not enough hundreds to subtract from.
Rename 1 thousand as 10 hundreds.

7,263 − 6,321 = _____

Piano B costs $_____ more than Piano A.

942 is close to 1,000.
The answer is reasonable.

Subtract the ones.

Th	H	T	O
7	2	6	3
− 6	3	2	1
			2

Subtract the tens.

Th	H	T	O
7	2	6	3
− 6	3	2	1
		4	2

Subtract the hundreds.

	6	12	
7̶	2̶	6	3
− 6	3	2	1
	9	4	2

Subtract the thousands.

	6	12	
7̶	2̶	6	3
− 6	3	2	1
	9	4	2

Activity!

USE TOOLS AND MODEL Use 💯 🔟 Ⅰ to show how you would find the difference between 5,134 and 2,716.

Learn Together

1. Subtract. You may use 💯 🔟 Ⅰ to help you.

   5,864 − 3,872 = _____

   Th H T O

     5 8 6 4
   − 3 8 7 2
   _____

2. Subtract.

   8,037 − 251 = _____

   Th H T O

     8 0 3 7
   −   2 5 1
   _____

Practice On Your Own

1. Find the difference. Show your work.

   (a) 8,452 – 6,327 = _____   **(b)** 5,382 – 547 = _____

   (c) 8,007 – 4,593 = _____   **(d)** 3,000 – 824 = _____

Think!

2. [CONSTRUCT VIABLE ARGUMENTS] Is this subtraction correct? Explain your thinking.

```
   8 3 0 2
 – 2 6 1 7
 ─────────
   6 3 1 5
```

2C Other Addition and Subtraction Strategies

59 **?**

+ 2

How would you add these numbers mentally?
(a) 59 and 2   **(b)** 64 and 20   **(c)** 382 and 200

Learn

(a) 59 + 2 = ?

59 + 2 = _____

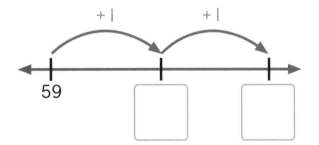

(b) 64 + 20 = ?

64 + 20 = _____

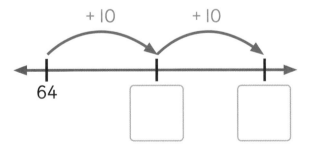

(c) 328 + 200 = ?

328 + 200 = _____

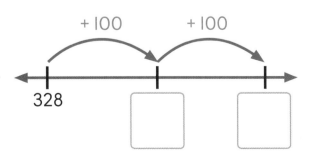

Learn Together

I. **(a)** 526 + 33 = ?

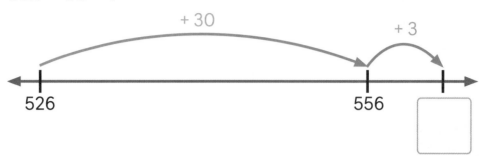

526 + 33 = _____

Count on by tens, then by ones.

(b) 526 + 233 = ?

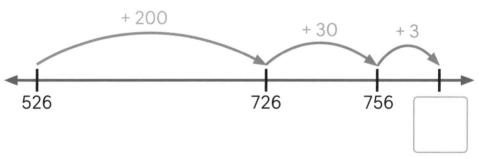

526 + 233 = _____

Practice On Your Own

I. Count on to add.

(a) 35 + 4 = _____

35 + 40 = _____

35 + 400 = _____

(b) 349 + 3 = _____

349 + 23 = _____

349 + 423 = _____

367 + 100 = ?
367 + 98 = ?

How would you add 367 and 98 mentally?

Learn

367 + 98 = ?

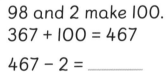

+100

− 2

367   465   467

367 + 98 = _____

98 and 2 make 100.
367 + 100 = 467
467 − 2 = _____

Learn Together

1.   247 + 95 = ?

+100

− 5

247   347

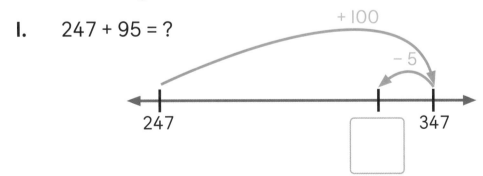

247 + 95 = _____

95 and _____ make 100.
247 + 100 = 347
347 − _____ = _____

2. 98 + 456 = ?

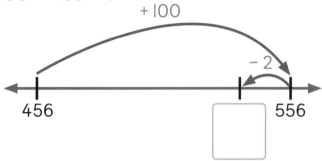

$+100$

-2

456   556

98 + 456 = _____

98 and _____ make 100.

100 + 456 = _____

_____ − _____ = _____

Practice On Your Own

I. Find the sum of 684 and 96. Show your work.

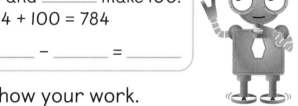

96 and _____ make 100.
684 + 100 = 784

_____ − _____ = _____

2. Find the sum of 198 and 254. Show your work.

3. USE STRUCTURE Show two ways to find the sum of 589 and 97.

How would you subtract these numbers mentally?

(a) 25 – 2

(b) 62 – 20

(c) 462 – 200

Learn

(a) 25 – 2 = ?

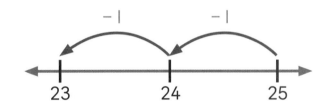

25 – 2 = _____

(b) 62 – 20 = ?

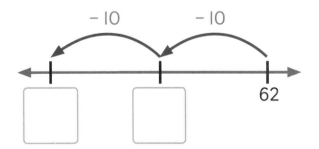

62 – 20 = _____

(c) 462 – 200 = ?

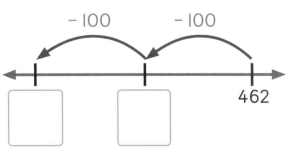

462 – 200 = _____

Learn Together

1. 927 − 22 = _____

Count back by tens, then by ones.

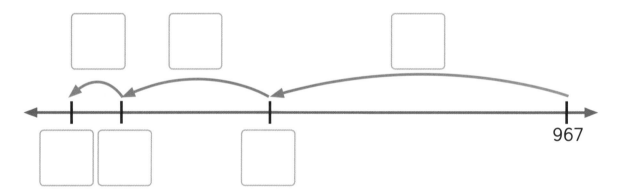

2. 967 − 53I = _____

Practice On Your Own

1. Count back to subtract.

(a) 5I7 − 4 = _____

(b) 649 − 3 = _____

5I7 − 40 = _____

649 − 43 = _____

5I7 − 400 = _____

649 − 243 = _____

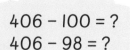

How would you subtract these numbers quickly?

406 − 100 = ?
406 − 98 = ?

Learn

406 − 98 = ?

− 100

+ 2

406

406 − 98 = _____

98 and 2 make 100.
406 − 100 = 306

306 + 2 = _____

Learn Together

1. 507 − 99 = ?

− 100

+ 1

507

507 − 99 = _____

99 and _____ make 100.

507 − 100 = _____

_____ + _____ = _____

2. 834 − 297 = ?

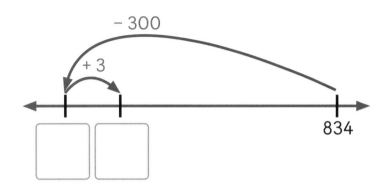

− 300

+ 3

834

834 − 297 = _____

297 and 3 make _____.

834 − _____ = _____

_____ + _____ = _____

Practice On Your Own

1. Find the difference between 708 and 96.
Show your work.

96 and _____ make 100.

708 − 100 = _____

_____ + _____ = _____

2. Find the difference between 900 and 398.
Show your work.

2D Word Problems

Mrs. Miller read 114 pages
of a book on Friday.
She read another 69 pages
of the book on Saturday.
The book had 200 pages.
How many pages did Mrs. Miller have left to read?

Learn

Step 1 **Draw a bar model to help you understand the problem.**

How many pages did Mrs. Miller have to read in all?

How many pages did she read on Friday and Saturday?

What do I have to find?

```
              200
   ┌──────────┴──────────┐
   │   Friday   │ Saturday │  │
   └──────┬─────┘────┬─────┘
        114         69
```

Solve.

First, find the number of pages Mrs. Miller read on Friday and Saturday.
Then, subtract the sum from the total number of pages of the book.

114 + 69 = _____

Mrs. Miller read _____ pages of the book on Friday and Saturday.

200 – _____ = _____

She had _____ pages of the book left to read.

Step 3 **Check.**

114 is close to _____.

69 is close to _____.

110 + 70 = _____

200 – _____ = _____

_____ is close to _____.

The answer is reasonable.

Learn Together

I. At a children's concert, there were 327 grandparents, 39l parents, and 568 children. How many people were there in all?

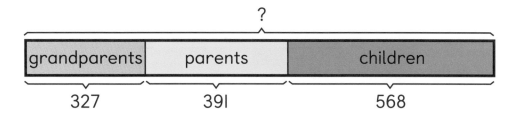

327 + 39l = _____

There were _____ grandparents and parents.

_____ + _____ = _____

There were _____ people in all.

2. A bread factory has 4,380 eggs. l,275 eggs are used to make plain rolls and l,369 eggs are used to make wheat rolls. How many eggs are there left?

4,380 − l,275 = _____

There are _____ eggs left after making the plain rolls.

_____ ◯ _____ = _____

There are _____ eggs left.

3. In a school, the third graders collected 768 cans for recycling. The fourth graders collected 85 fewer cans than the third graders. The fifth graders collected 163 more cans than the fourth graders. How many cans did the fifth graders collect?

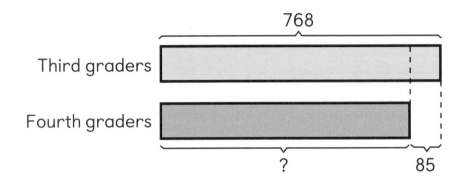

768 − 85 = _____

The fourth graders collected _____ cans.

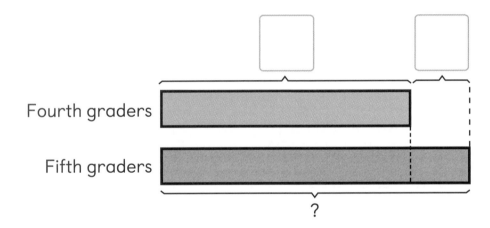

_____ ◯ _____ = _____

The fifth graders collected _____ cans.

4. Town A had 4,712 people. After 628 people moved out of Town A, there were 1,259 fewer people in Town A than Town B. How many people did Town B have?

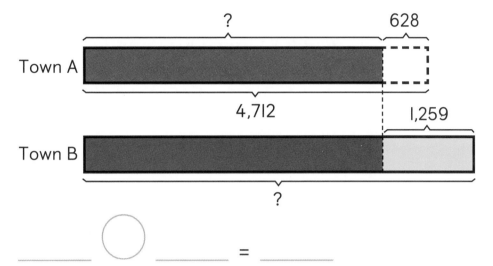

_____ $\bigcirc$ _____ = _____

There were _____ people left in Town A.

_____ $\bigcirc$ _____ = _____

Town B had _____ people.

5. The third graders collected 3,196 bottles for recycling. Of the bottles collected, 758 were glass and the rest were plastic. How many bottles were plastic?

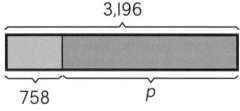

$758 + p = 3{,}196$

$p = 3{,}196 \bigcirc 758$

= _____

> p stands for the number of plastic bottles.

_____ bottles were plastic.

Practice On Your Own 📝

Solve. Draw bar models to help you.

1. Mr. Jones owns a ranch. He has 429 cows. He has 295 more chickens than cows. How many cows and chickens does Mr. Jones have in all?

Mr. Jones has _____ cows and chickens in all.

2. Machine A makes 3,194 jars of honey. Machine B makes 427 more jars of honey than Machine A. Machine C makes 203 more jars of honey than Machine B. How many jars of honey does Machine C make?

Machine C makes _____ jars of honey.

3. There were 743 passengers on a subway when it left Bryant Park station for Grand Central station. At Grand Central station, 261 passengers got off and 159 passengers boarded the subway. How many passengers were on the subway when it left Grand Central station?

There were _____ people on the subway when it left Grand Central station.

4. There were 6,531 adults at a football stadium. After another 1,072 more adults entered the stadium, there were 5,967 more adults than children. How many children were there?

There were _____ children.

5. Mr. Cruz is selling coupons for a carnival. He has 2,745 food coupons and some game coupons. He sells 639 of the food coupons. Now he has 1,372 more food coupons than game coupons left. How many game coupons does he have?

He has _____ game coupons.

Think!

6. PERSEVERE Noah was thinking of a number. He subtracted 237, and then added 1,083 to the number. He got 4,792. What number did Noah start with?

Noah started with _____.

Performance Task

The tallest building in each continent in 2019 is shown below.

Tallest Buildings in Each Continent in 2019

Burj Khalifa in Asia	2,717 feet
The Leonardo in Africa	745 feet
One World Trade Center in North America	1,776 feet
Gran Torre Santiago in South America	980 feet
Long Duration Balloon (LDB) Payload Preparation in Antarctica	49 feet
Lakhta Center in Europe	1,516 feet
QI in Oceania	1,060 feet

1. (a) What was the tallest building in the world in 2019?

_____

(b) REASON Can you say that One World Trade Center was the second tallest building in the world in 2019? Explain your answer.

2. How much taller is the Lakhta Center than The Leonardo? Show your work.

The Lakhta Center is _____ feet taller than The Leonardo.

3. REASON The height of One World Trade Center is taller than the total heights of The Leonardo and Gran Torre Santiago. Do you agree? Explain your answer.

4. **(a)** The height of QI in Oceania is made up of the height of its spire and its roof height. The height of its spire is 254 feet. What is the roof height of QI?

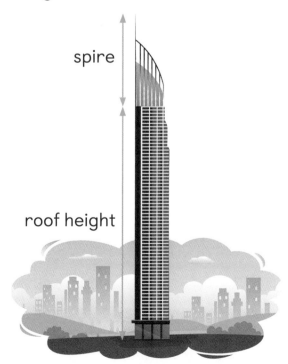

The roof height of QI

is _____ feet.

(b) REASON Explain how you can check if the answer in **(a)** is reasonable.

5. REASON AND MODEL The difference in height between two of the buildings is 1,737 feet. Which are the two buildings? Show your work.

How Did I Do?

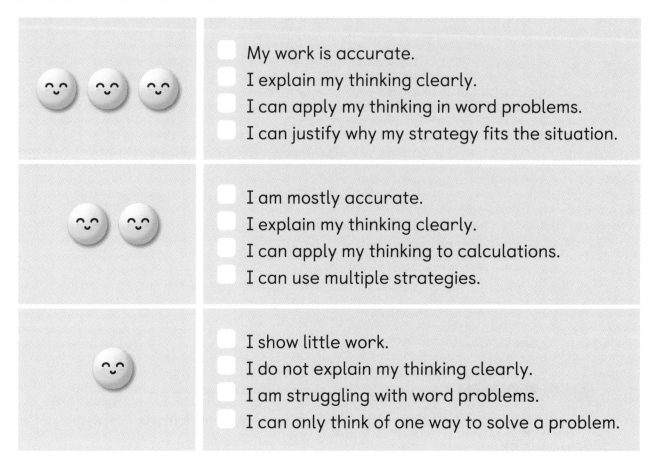

- My work is accurate.
- I explain my thinking clearly.
- I can apply my thinking in word problems.
- I can justify why my strategy fits the situation.

- I am mostly accurate.
- I explain my thinking clearly.
- I can apply my thinking to calculations.
- I can use multiple strategies.

- I show little work.
- I do not explain my thinking clearly.
- I am struggling with word problems.
- I can only think of one way to solve a problem.

My Teacher's Words

Chapter Practice

I. Which pair of numbers makes 5,000?

    Ⓐ 1,265 and 2,735   Ⓑ 3,697 and 1,303

    Ⓒ 259 and 2,741   Ⓓ 2,381 and 2,620

2. Mr. Brown has 4,365 oranges. He sells 3,679 oranges. How many oranges does he have left?

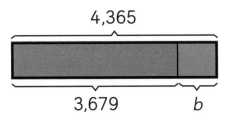

    Ⓐ 1,314   Ⓑ 8,044

    Ⓒ 6,860   Ⓓ 686

3. 134 + 459 = _____

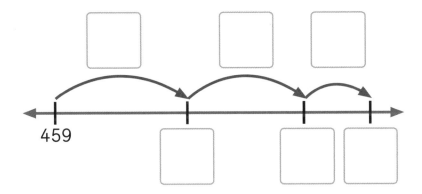

4. Find the difference between 800 and 498.

5. Find the sum. Show your work.

    (a) 6,318 + 3,271 = _____

    (b) 3,516 + 728 = _____

    (c) 5,189 + 611 = _____

    (d) 4,753 + 4,247 = _____

6. Find the difference. Show your work.

    (a) 9,562 – 6,341 = _____

    (b) 5,871 – 246 = _____

(c) 7,249 – 6,257 = _____ **(d)** 4,000 – 372 = _____

7. James earns 2,673 points in the first round of a video game.
He earns 3,108 points in the second round of the game.
He earns 1,495 points in the third round of the game.
How many points does James earn in all?

James earns _____ points in all.

8. There were 5,612 cars at the parking area of a mall.
After 1,078 cars left the parking area, another 2,439 cars
parked there. How many cars were there after that?

There were _____ cars after that.

9. **REASON** Circle the bar model that best shows the word problem below. Explain your answer.

A cookie factory bakes 3,076 cookies in the morning. The factory bakes another 2,254 cookies in the afternoon. How many cookies does the cookie factory bake in all?

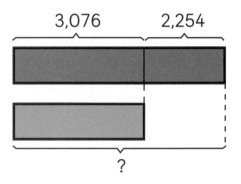

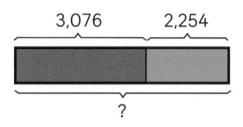

10. **PERSEVERE** Find the missing digits.

$$
\begin{array}{r}
3\ \boxed{?}\ \boxed{?}\ 2 \\
-\ \boxed{?}\ 2\ 5\ \boxed{?} \\
\hline
2\ 3\ 4\ 5
\end{array}
$$

Chapter

3 MULTIPLICATION AND DIVISION

Ms. Cruz wants to buy all the pencils.

How can you find out how many pencils she buys?

How can Ms. Cruz share all the pencils equally among 10 students in her reading group?

Recall

1. How many pairs can you make?

(A) 1   (B) 2

(C) 4   (D) 8

2. Write the missing numbers.

6 groups of _____

5 + 5 + 5 + 5 + 5 + 5 = _____

6 fives = _____

3. How many stickers are there in all?

3 rows of _____

_____ + _____ + _____ = _____

There are _____ stickers in all.

I can...

☐ pair objects.

☐ find the total
   number in equal
   groups using
   repeated addition.

☐ find the total
   number using
   rectangular arrays.

3A Multiplication

Peter buys 3 packs of erasers.
Each pack has 2 erasers.
How many erasers does he buy in all?

3 equal groups
of erasers

Learn

3 groups of 2

3 × 2 = 6 is a **multiplication equation**.

You **multiply (×)** to find the total number.

3 × 2 = 2 + 2 + 2

= _____

Peter buys _____ erasers in all.

Learn Together

1. How many pens are there altogether?

2 groups of 3
3 + 3

$2 \times 3 =$ _____

There are _____ pens altogether.

2. How many magnets are there in all?

_____ groups of 5
5 + 5 + 5

_____ $\times 5 =$ _____

There are _____ magnets in all.

3. How many colored pencils are there altogether?

$5 \times$ _____ $=$ _____

There are _____ colored pencils altogether.

Practice on Your Own

I. How many toy planes are there in all?

_____ × 7 = _____

There are _____ toy planes in all.

2. How many books are there altogether?

4 × _____ = _____

There are _____ books altogether.

3. Ravi buys 3 boxes of bagels.
   Each box has 5 bagels.
   How many bagels does he buy altogether?

_____ × _____ = _____

He buys _____ bagels altogether.

Think!

4. REASON Is it possible to write a multiplication equation for the three boxes of dolls? Explain your answer.

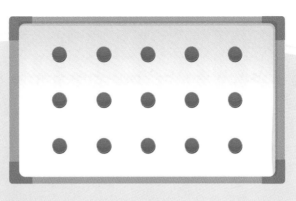

How can you find the total number of magnets?

Learn

The **array** shows 3 **rows** of 5.

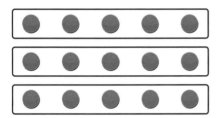

3 groups of 5

$3 \times 5 = 5 + 5 + 5$

$\quad = $ _____

There are _____ magnets in all.

The array shows 5 **columns** of 3.

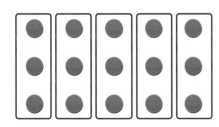

5 groups of 3

$5 \times 3 = 3 + 3 + 3 + 3 + 3$

$\quad = $ _____

There are _____ magnets in all.

Activity!

MODEL Use to show 2 × 5. Your classmate shows 5 × 2.
Draw to show 2 × 5 and 5 × 2. Discuss what you notice.

Learn Together

I. Write the missing numbers.

2 × 4 = _____   4 × 2 = _____

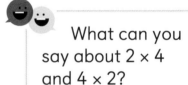

What can you say about 2 × 4 and 4 × 2?

2. Write the missing numbers.

3 × _____ = _____

7 × _____ = _____

Is 3 × 7 equal to 7 × 3?

Practice On Your Own 📝

I. There are 2 rows of chairs.
    There are 6 chairs in each row.
    How many chairs are there in all?

_____ × _____ = _____

There are _____ chairs in all.

2. The trees are planted in 2 rows.
    There are 10 trees in each row.
    How many trees are there altogether?

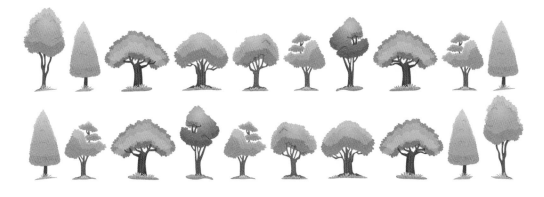

_____ × _____ = _____

There are _____ trees altogether.

3. How many flags are there in all?

_____ × _____ = _____

There are _____ flags in all.

4. USE STRUCTURE Write the missing numbers.

●●●●
●●●●
●●●●

_____ × _____ = _____

_____ × _____ = _____

3 × _____ = 4 × _____

3B Multiply by 2

Use two ways to find the number of mittens there are in all.

Learn

Count by twos.

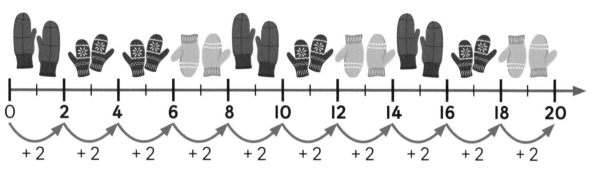

$10 \times 2 =$ _____

There are _____ mittens in all.

2, 4, 6, ..., 16, 18, 20

10 twos = _____

Learn Together

1. How many socks are there in 8 pairs?

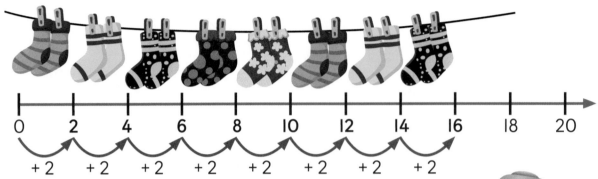

$8 \times 2 =$ _____

2, 4, 6, ...

There are _____ socks in 8 pairs.

2. How many peaches are there in all?

$5 \times 2 =$ _____

Count by 2s.

There are _____ peaches in all.

3. How many chairs are there altogether?

_____ $\times 9 =$ _____

There are _____ chairs altogether.

4. Multiply 2 by 3.

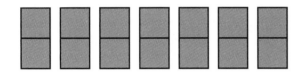

$2 \times 3 =$ _____

Add 2 three times.

5. Multiply 2 by 7.

_____ × _____ = _____

What is the multiplication equation for 0 groups of 2? Explain your answer.

Practice On Your Own 📝

I. How many lemons are there in all?

_____ × 2 = _____

There are _____ lemons in all.

2. How many toy cars are there altogether?

_____ × _____ = _____

There are _____ toy cars altogether.

3. Multiply 2 by 5.

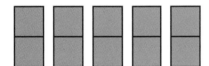

_____ × _____ = _____

4. Multiply 2 by 10.

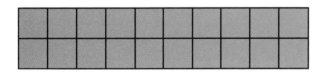

_____ × _____ = _____

5. Circle groups of 2.
Then write a multiplication equation.

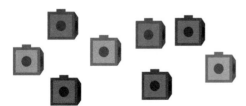

_____ × _____ = _____

Learn

$\left.\begin{array}{c}\bullet\bullet\bullet\bullet\bullet \\ \bullet\bullet\bullet\bullet\bullet\end{array}\right\} 2 \times 5$

$2 \times 5 = $ _____

$\left.\begin{array}{c}\bullet\bullet\bullet\bullet\bullet\bullet \\ \bullet\bullet\bullet\bullet\bullet\bullet\end{array}\right\} 2 \times 6$

$2 \times 6 = $ _____

Double 6 is 2 more than double 5.

Learn Together

1. Double 3 is 6.

    $2 \times 3 =$ _____

What is double 4?

    $2 \times 4 =$ _____

2 more

2. What are double 7 and double 6?

$2 \times 7 =$ _____ $2 \times 6 =$ _____

2 less

Activity!

USE TOOLS AND MODEL Roll two  until you get a double. Draw the double and write a multiplication equation.

Practice On Your Own

I. **(a)** What is double 10?

$2 \times 10 =$ _____

(b) What is double 9?

$2 \times 9 =$ _____

2. Write the missing numbers.

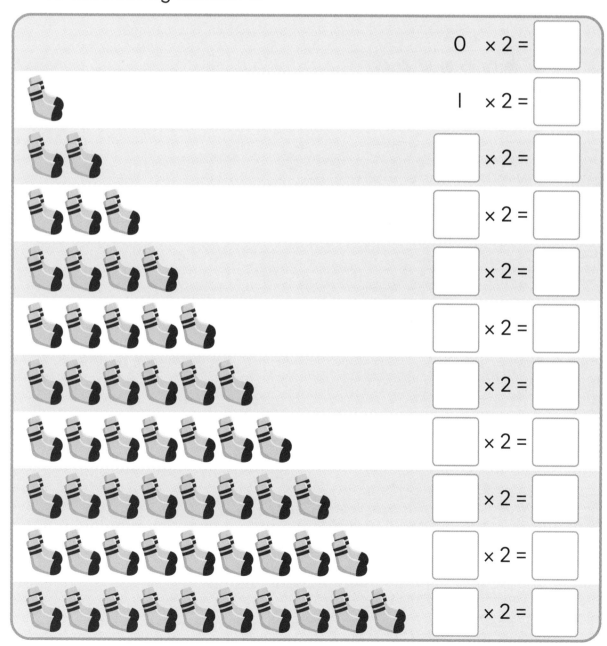

$0 \quad \times 2 =$ ☐

$1 \quad \times 2 =$ ☐

☐ $\times 2 =$ ☐

☐ $\times 2 =$ ☐

☐ $\times 2 =$ ☐

☐ $\times 2 =$ ☐

☐ $\times 2 =$ ☐

☐ $\times 2 =$ ☐

☐ $\times 2 =$ ☐

☐ $\times 2 =$ ☐

☐ $\times 2 =$ ☐

Think!

3. Look at the pattern.

$2 \times 2 = 4$

$2 \times 4 = 8$

$2 \times 8 = 16$

What is 2×16? Explain your thinking.

3C Multiply by 5

How many crayons are there altogether?
How do you find your answer?

Learn

Count by fives.

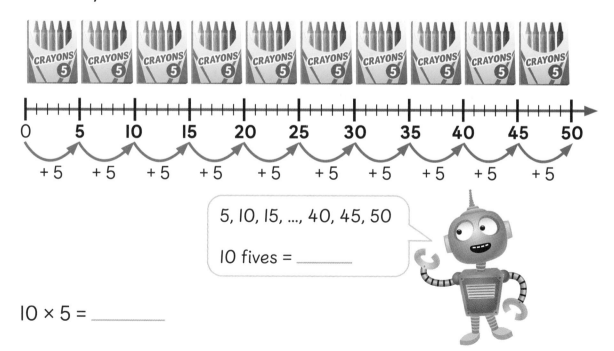

5, 10, 15, ..., 40, 45, 50

10 fives = _____

10 × 5 = _____

There are _____ crayons altogether.

Learn Together

1. How many crayons are there in 5 boxes?

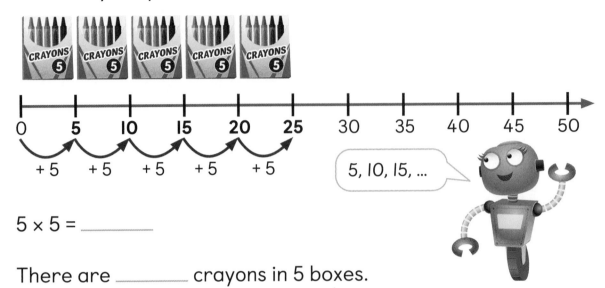

5, 10, 15, ...

$5 \times 5 =$ _____

There are _____ crayons in 5 boxes.

Does skip counting start from 0? Explain your answer.

2. How many stars are there in all?

$3 \times 5 =$ _____

Count by 5s.

There are _____ stars in all.

Name: _____ Date: _____

3. How many baseball caps are there in all?

_____ × 5 = _____

There are _____ baseball caps in all.

4. How many toy planes are there altogether?

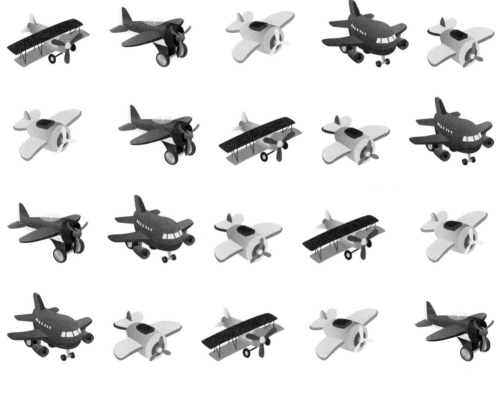

_____ × _____ = _____

There are _____ toy planes altogether.

5. Multiply 5 by 7.

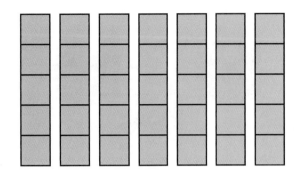

_____ × _____ = _____

Practice On Your Own ✍️

I. How many ping-pong balls are there in all?

_____ × 5 = _____

There are _____ ping-pong balls in all.

2. How many kites are there altogether?

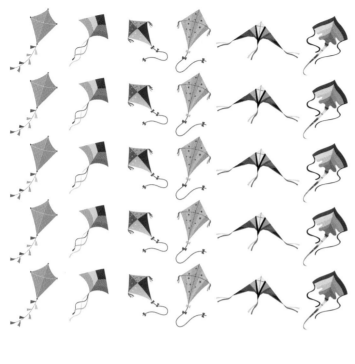

_____ × _____ = _____

There are _____ kites altogether.

3. Multiply 5 by 4.

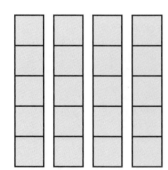   _____ × _____ = _____

4. Multiply.

   _____ × _____ = _____

5. Circle groups of 5.
Then write a multiplication equation.

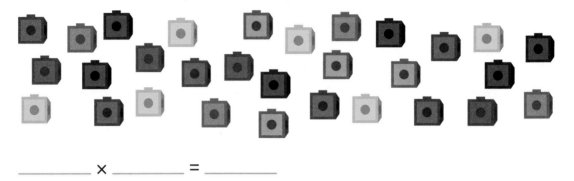

_____ × _____ = _____

6. Write the missing numbers.

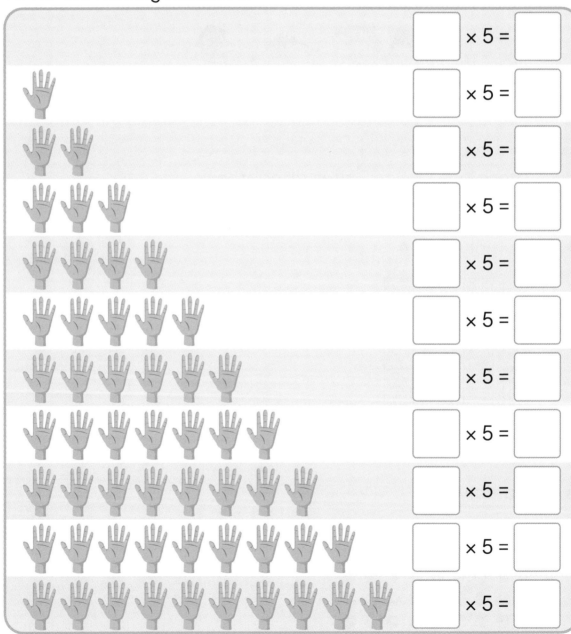

3D Multiply by 10

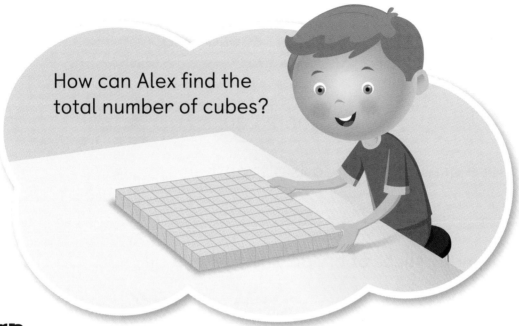

How can Alex find the total number of cubes?

Learn

Count by tens.

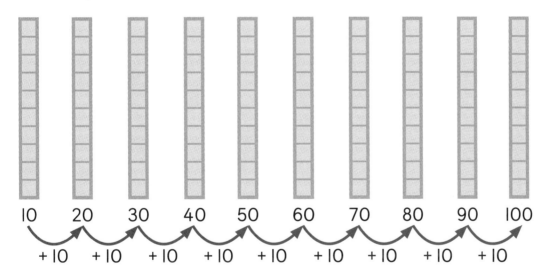

| 10 | 20 | 30 | 40 | 50 | 60 | 70 | 80 | 90 | 100 |

+ 10   + 10   + 10   + 10   + 10   + 10   + 10   + 10   + 10

$10 \times 10 =$ _____

There are _____ cubes in all.

10 tens = 1 hundred

Learn Together

1. How many beads are there altogether?

$7 \times 10 =$ _____

10, 20, 30, ...

There are _____ beads altogether.

2. How many slices of bread are there in all?

_____ $\times 10 =$ _____

Count by 10s.

There are _____ slices of bread in all.

3. Multiply.

_____ $\times$ _____ $=$ _____

4. Write the missing numbers.

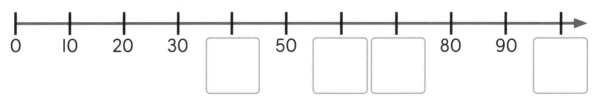

Practice On Your Own

1. How many bowling pins are there in all?

_____ × 10 = _____

There are _____ bowling pins in all.

2. How much money is there?

_____ × _____ = _____

There is $_____.

3. Multiply.

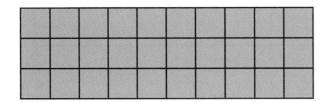   _____ × _____ = _____

4. Circle groups of 10.
Then write a multiplication equation.

   _____ × _____

= _____

Think!

5. LOOK FOR PATTERNS This is a multiplication chart.

(a) Write the missing numbers.

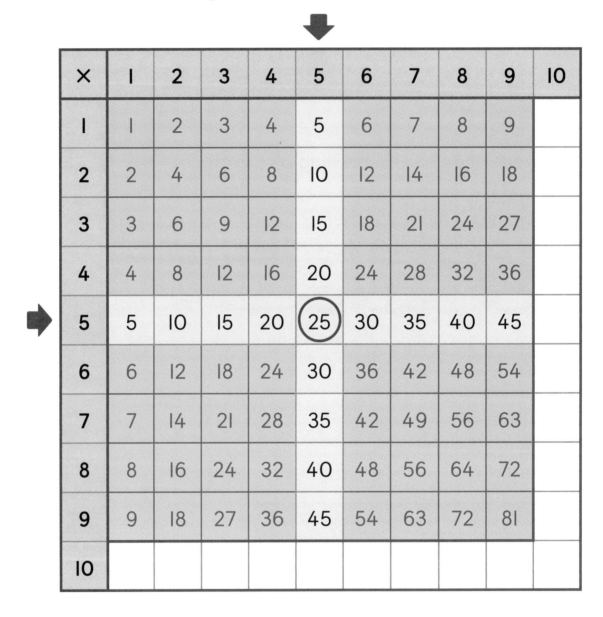

×	1	2	3	4	5	6	7	8	9	10
1	1	2	3	4	5	6	7	8	9	
2	2	4	6	8	10	12	14	16	18	
3	3	6	9	12	15	18	21	24	27	
4	4	8	12	16	20	24	28	32	36	
5	5	10	15	20	(25)	30	35	40	45	
6	6	12	18	24	30	36	42	48	54	
7	7	14	21	28	35	42	49	56	63	
8	8	16	24	32	40	48	56	64	72	
9	9	18	27	36	45	54	63	72	81	
10										

(b) Look at the multiplication facts of 5 and 10 in the chart. What patterns do you see?

3E Multiply by 3

How many wheels does a tricycle have?
How many wheels are there in all?

Learn

Count by threes.

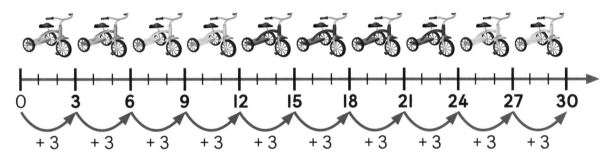

3, 6, 9, ..., 24, 27, 30

10 threes = _____

10 × 3 = _____

There are _____ wheels in all.

Learn Together

1. How many wheels are there on 4 rollerblades?

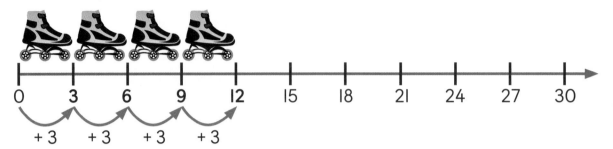

$4 \times 3 =$ _____

There are _____ wheels on 4 rollerblades.

2. Multiply.

$3 \times 4 =$ _____ $4 \times 3 =$ _____ $3 \times 4 = 4 \times 3$

3. Multiply.

$8 \times 3 =$ _____ $3 \times 8 =$ _____

4. Multiply.

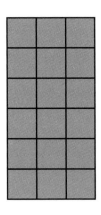

$6 \times 3 =$ _____

$3 \times 6 =$ _____

Practice On Your Own

1. How many fish are there in all?

_____ $\times 3 =$ _____

There are _____ fish in all.

2. How many triangles are there altogether?

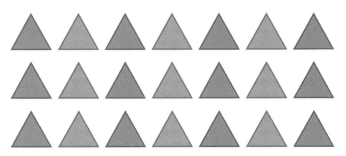

_____ $\times$ _____ $=$ _____

There are _____ triangles altogether.

3. Write two multiplication equations.

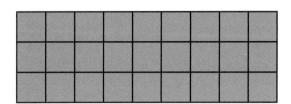

_____ × _____ = _____

_____ × _____ = _____

4. **(a)** Circle groups of 3.
Then write a multiplication equation.

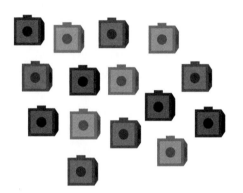

_____ × _____ = _____

(b) Circle groups of 5.
Then write a multiplication equation.

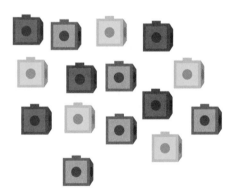

_____ × _____ = _____

(c) Write the missing numbers.

_____ × _____ = _____ × _____

Learn

5 groups of 3
5 × 3 = 15

6 groups of 3

6 × 3 = 15 + _____

= _____

3 more

Learn Together

Write the missing numbers.

1.

$5 \times 3 = 15$ $7 \times 3 = 15 +$ _____

                            $=$ _____

2.

3 fives

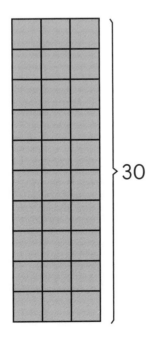

3 fours

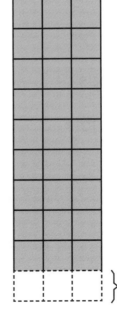

$3 \times 5 =$ _____ $3 \times 4 =$ _____

3 less

3.

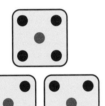

$10 \times 3 = 30$

$9 \times 3 = 30 -$ _____

$=$ _____

Activity!

MODEL You know that $3 \times 10 = 30$. Discuss with your classmate how you would use 3×10 to find 3×8. Use to show how.

> Discuss with your classmate how you would use 3×10 to find 3×11.

Practice On Your Own

Write the missing numbers.

1.  $3 \times 5 = 15$

 $3 \times 4 = 15$ ◯ _____

   = _____

 $3 \times 6 = 15$ ◯ _____

   = _____

2.

$3 \times 5 = 15$

$3 \times 7 = 15 \bigcirc \underline{\hspace{3cm}}$

$= \underline{\hspace{3cm}}$

3.

$0 \times 3 = \underline{\hspace{2cm}}$	$3 \times 0 = \underline{\hspace{2cm}}$
$1 \times 3 = \underline{\hspace{2cm}}$	$3 \times 1 = \underline{\hspace{2cm}}$
$2 \times 3 = \underline{\hspace{2cm}}$	$3 \times 2 = \underline{\hspace{2cm}}$
$3 \times 3 = \underline{\hspace{2cm}}$	$3 \times \underline{\hspace{2cm}} = 9$
$4 \times 3 = \underline{\hspace{2cm}}$	$3 \times \underline{\hspace{2cm}} = 12$
$5 \times 3 = \underline{\hspace{2cm}}$	$3 \times \underline{\hspace{2cm}} = 15$
$6 \times 3 = \underline{\hspace{2cm}}$	$3 \times \underline{\hspace{2cm}} = 18$
$7 \times 3 = \underline{\hspace{2cm}}$	$3 \times \underline{\hspace{2cm}} = 21$
$8 \times 3 = \underline{\hspace{2cm}}$	$3 \times \underline{\hspace{2cm}} = 24$
$9 \times 3 = \underline{\hspace{2cm}}$	$3 \times \underline{\hspace{2cm}} = 27$
$10 \times 3 = \underline{\hspace{2cm}}$	$3 \times \underline{\hspace{2cm}} = 30$

3F Multiply by 4

How many vehicles are there?
How many wheels are there in all?

Learn

Count by fours.

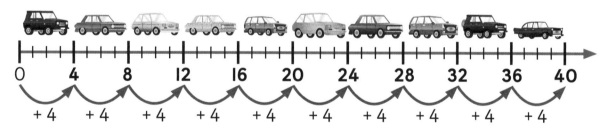

| 0 | 4 | 8 | 12 | 16 | 20 | 24 | 28 | 32 | 36 | 40 |

+ 4 + 4 + 4 + 4 + 4 + 4 + 4 + 4 + 4 + 4

4, 8, 12, ..., 32, 36, 40

$10 \times 4 =$ _____

10 fours = _____

There are _____ wheels in all.

Learn Together

1. How many wheels are there on 5 cars?

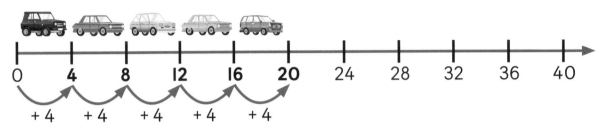

$5 \times 4 =$ _____

There are _____ wheels on 5 cars.

2. Multiply.

$4 \times 5 =$ _____ $5 \times 4 =$ _____ $4 \times 5 = 5 \times 4$

3. Multiply.

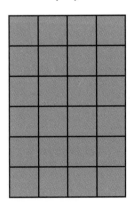

$6 \times 4 =$ _____

$4 \times 6 =$ _____

Practice On Your Own

Write the missing numbers.

1.

_____ × _____ = _____

There are _____ keys in all.

2.

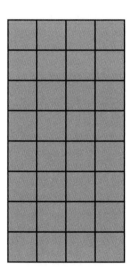

_____ × _____ = _____

_____ × _____ = _____

3.

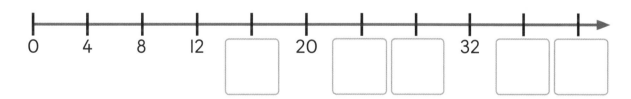

4.

0 × 4 = _____	4 × 0 = _____
1 × 4 = _____	4 × 1 = _____
2 × 4 = _____	4 × 2 = _____
3 × 4 = _____	4 × _____ = _____
4 × 4 = _____	4 × _____ = _____
5 × 4 = _____	4 × _____ = _____
6 × 4 = _____	4 × _____ = _____
7 × 4 = _____	4 × _____ = _____
8 × 4 = _____	4 × _____ = _____
9 × 4 = _____	4 × _____ = _____
10 × 4 = _____	4 × _____ = _____

Think!

5. REASON 5 × 4 is 4 less than 6 × 4.

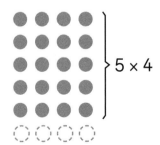

5 × 4

Is 4 × 5 also 4 less than 4 × 6?
Explain your answer.

5 × 4 = ?
4 × 4 = ?

Daniel arranges his cards in an array. How is 4 × 4 related to 5 × 4?

Learn

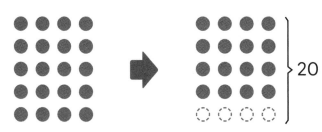

5 groups of 4

5 × 4 = 20

4 groups of 4

4 × 4 = 20 − _____

= _____

4 less

Learn Together

Write the missing numbers.

1.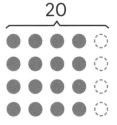

20

$4 \times 5 = 20$

$4 \times 4 = 20 - \underline{\hspace{2cm}}$

$= \underline{\hspace{2cm}}$

4 less

2. 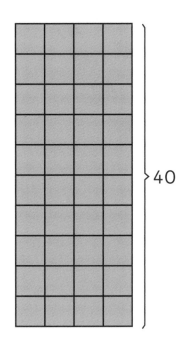 40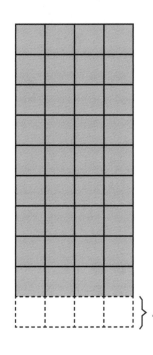

$10 \times 4 = 40$

$9 \times 4 = 40 - \underline{\hspace{2cm}}$

$= \underline{\hspace{2cm}}$

} 4

3.

8×4

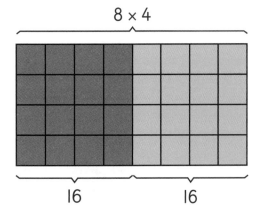

16   16

$4 \times 4 = 16$

$8 \times 4 = \underline{\hspace{2cm}} + \underline{\hspace{2cm}}$

$= \underline{\hspace{2cm}}$

 What other strategies can you use to find 8×4?

4.

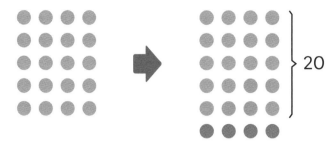

$5 \times 4 = 20$ $6 \times 4 = 20 +$ _____

                      $=$ _____

5.

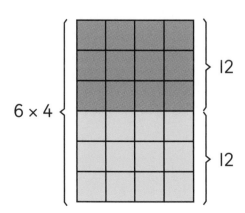

$2 \times 4 = 8$

$6 \times 4 =$ _____ $+$ _____ $+$ _____

        $=$ _____

6.

$3 \times 4 = 12$

$6 \times 4 =$ _____ $+$ _____

        $=$ _____

Practice On Your Own

Write the missing numbers.

1.  $4 \times 5 = 20$

    $4 \times 6 = 20$ ◯ _____

               = _____

   $4 \times 4 = 20$ ◯ _____

               = _____

2.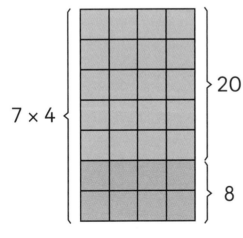

   $5 \times 4 =$ _____

   $2 \times 4 =$ _____

   $7 \times 4 =$ _____ ◯ _____

            = _____

3G Word Problems

A chef bakes 2 pizzas.
He cuts each pizza into 8 slices.
How many slices of pizza are
there in all?

Learn

Step 1   **Draw a bar model to help you understand the problem.**

How many pizzas are there?
How many slices are there in each
pizza? What do I have to find?

?

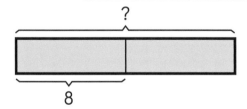

8

Step 2   **Solve.**

$2 \times 8 =$ _____

There are _____ slices of pizza in all.

Step 3   **Check.**

$8 + 8 =$ _____

The answer is correct.

Learn Together

1. Ella packs 5 boxes of granola bars for her friends. There are 3 granola bars in each box. How many granola bars are there in all?

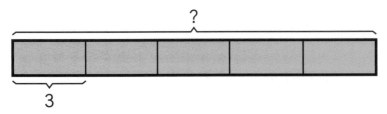

$5 \times 3 =$ _____

There are _____ granola bars in all.

2. Nick has 6 stacks of books. There are 4 books in each stack. How many books are there in all?

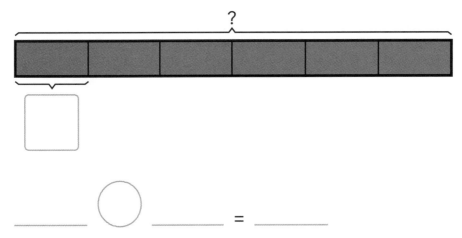

_____ ◯ _____ = _____

There are _____ books in all.

3. Mrs. Wilson buys 5 bags of potatoes. There are 10 potatoes in each bag. How many potatoes does she buy in all?

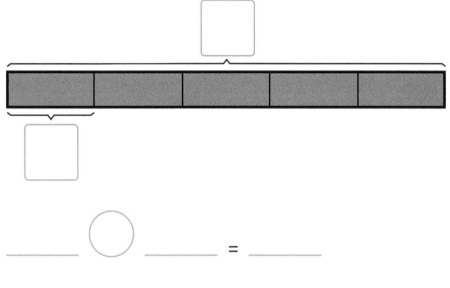

_____ ◯ _____ = _____

She buys _____ potatoes in all.

Practice On Your Own

Solve. Show your work.

1. A restaurant has 5 tables. There are 2 customers sitting at each table. How many customers are there in all?

There are _____ customers in all.

2. Mr. Moore buys 3 bunches of carrots. There are 9 carrots in each bunch. How many carrots does he buy?

He buys _____ carrots.

3. A building has 7 floors. Each floor has 10 offices. How many offices are there in all?

There are _____ offices in all.

Think!

4. REASON Juan has 3 boxes of 6 pencils each. Zoe has 6 boxes of 3 pencils each. Who has more pencils? Explain your answer.

3H Division

3 children share 6 sandwiches equally.
How many sandwiches does each child get?

Learn

Divide 6 sandwiches equally into 3 groups.

You divide (÷) to find the number in each group.

$6 \div 3 =$ _____ $6 \div 3 = 2$ is a **division equation**.

Each child gets _____ sandwiches.

Activity!

USE TOOLS AND MODEL Use 18 📷 to build 3 equal stacks. Write a division equation to show the number of 📷 in each stack.

Learn Together

1. Share 8 muffins equally among 4 children.
   Draw circles to show how many muffins each child gets.

$8 \div 4 =$ _____

$4 \times$ _____ $= 8$

Each child gets _____ muffins.

2. Share 12 oranges equally among 3 children.
Draw circles to show how many oranges each child gets.

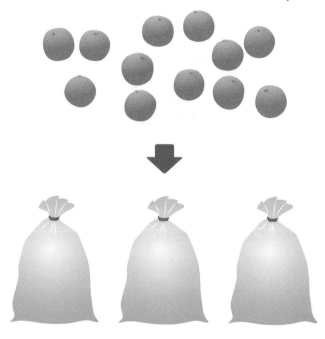

12 ÷ 3 = _____

Each child gets _____ oranges.

3. The stickers are arranged as shown.

There are 15 stickers in _____ rows.

15 ÷ _____ = _____

Each row has _____ stickers.

Practice On Your Own

1. Divide 12 toy cars into 4 equal groups.

12 ÷ 4 = _____

There are _____ toy cars in each group.

2. Divide 20 strawberries into 4 equal groups.

20 ÷ 4 = _____

There are _____ strawberries in each group.

3. Draw 14 stars arranged equally into 2 rows.

_____ ◯ _____ = _____

Each row has _____ stars.

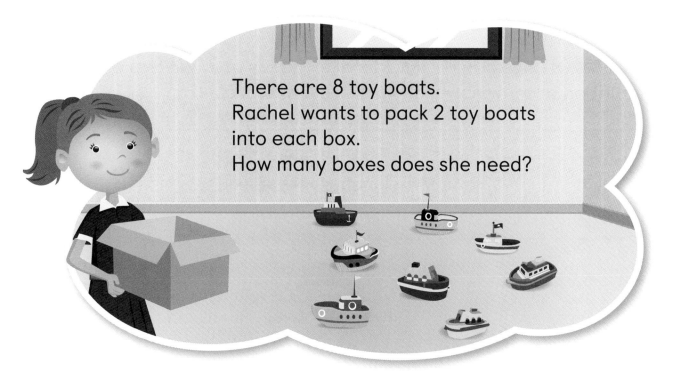

Learn

Divide 8 toy boats into groups of 2.

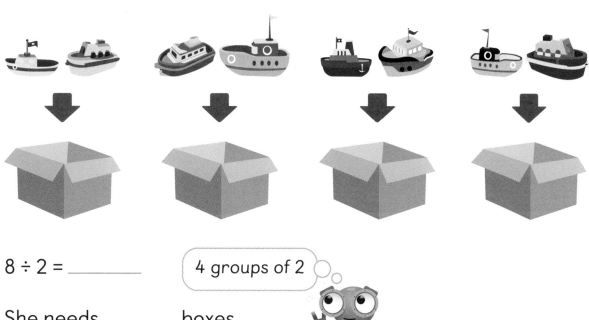

$8 \div 2 =$ _____   4 groups of 2

She needs _____ boxes.

Activity!

USE TOOLS AND MODEL Use 12 to make groups of 2. Write a division equation to show how many groups there are.

Explain to your classmate how division is related to muliplication.

Learn Together

1. Divide 12 oranges into groups of 4.

12 ÷ 4 = _____

 _____ × 4 = 12

There are _____ groups.

2. Circle groups of 3.

18 ÷ 3 = _____

There are _____ groups.

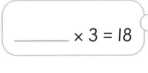 _____ × 3 = 18

3.   Mr. Carter has $10. He gives $5 to each of his children.
How many children does Mr. Carter have?

10 ÷ 5 = _____

Mr. Carter has _____ children.

4.   The length of a piece of ribbon is 6 meters. Levi cuts the ribbon
into equal pieces, each 2 meters long. How many pieces of
ribbon does he have?

| 2 meters | 2 meters | 2 meters |

6 ÷ 2 = _____

He has _____ pieces of ribbon.

Practice On Your Own

1.   Divide 24 beads into groups of 4.

24 ÷ 4 = _____

There are _____ groups.

2. Carla cuts an 18-foot rope into 6-foot pieces.
How many pieces of rope does she have?

18 feet

18 ÷ 6 = _____

She has _____ pieces of rope.

3. Eva has 14 pine cones.
She puts 7 pine cones in each box.
How many boxes does she need?

_____ ÷ _____ = _____

She needs _____ boxes.

31 Divide by 2

Share 6 stickers equally between 2 children.

Learn

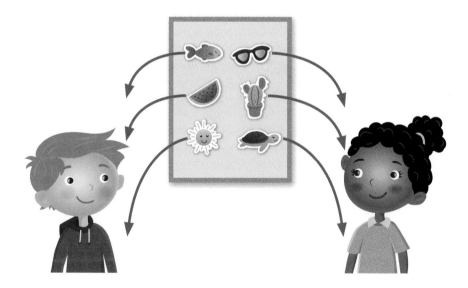

6 ÷ 2 = _____

Each child gets _____ stickers.

 What does 6 ÷ 2 mean? Explain your answer.

Learn Together

1. Put 10 pencils equally into 2 pencil holders.

$10 \div 2 =$ _____

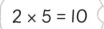 $2 \times 5 = 10$

There are _____ pencils in each pencil holder.

2.

_____ groups of 2

_____ $\times 2 = 6$

$6 \div 2 =$ _____

2 groups of _____

$2 \times$ _____ $= 6$

$6 \div 2 =$ _____

3.

$2 \times$ _____ $= 8$

$8 \div 2 =$ _____

4. (a)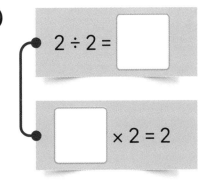

$2 \div 2 =$ ☐

☐ $\times 2 = 2$

(b)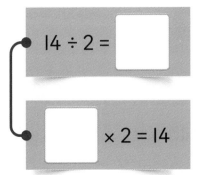

$14 \div 2 =$ ☐

☐ $\times 2 = 14$

Activity!

USE TOOLS AND MODEL Use to show each set below.

Set A: 4 groups of 2   Set B: 5 groups of 2

Draw the sets. Then write as many multiplication and division equations as you can.

Practice On Your Own

Write the missing numbers.

1.   Put 16 shells equally into 2 boxes.

16 ÷ 2 = _____

There are _____ shells in each box.

2.

_____ groups of 2

_____ × 2 = 10

10 ÷ 2 = _____

2 groups of _____

2 × _____ = 10

10 ÷ 2 = _____

3. **(a)**

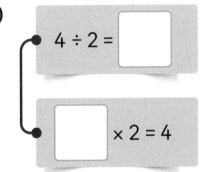

4 ÷ 2 = [ ]

[ ] × 2 = 4

(b)

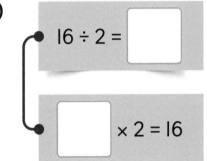

16 ÷ 2 = [ ]

[ ] × 2 = 16

4. There are 10 shoes.
How many pairs of shoes are there?

10 ÷ _____ = _____

There are _____ pairs of shoes.

3J Divide by 5

Put 15 muffins equally into 5 boxes.
How many muffins will each box have?

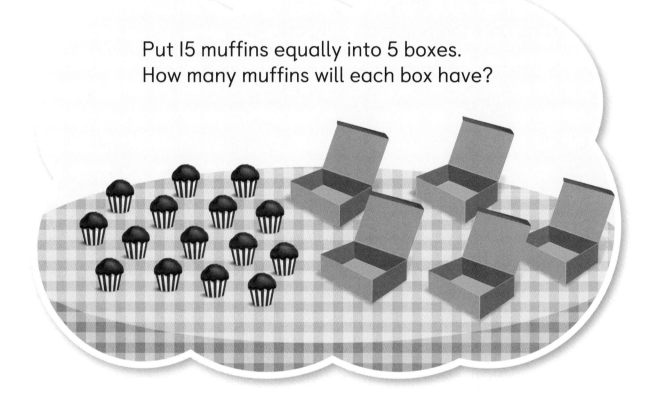

Learn

15 ÷ 5 = _____

Each box will have _____ muffins.

Activity!

USE TOOLS AND MODEL Use 10 📷 to make equal groups. Draw the groups. Then write as many multiplication and division equations as you can using only the numbers 2, 5, and 10.

Learn Together

I. Put 20 muffins equally into 5 boxes.

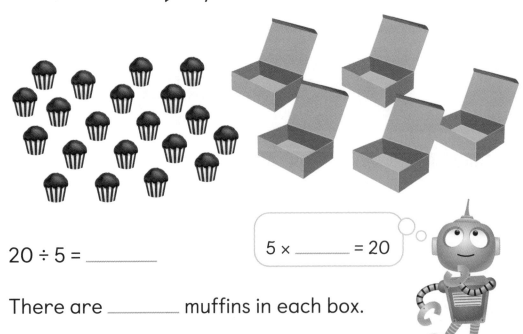

20 ÷ 5 = _____

5 × _____ = 20

There are _____ muffins in each box.

2.

_____ groups of 5   5 groups of _____

_____ × 5 = 20   5 × _____ = 20

20 ÷ 5 = _____   20 ÷ 5 = _____

Practice On Your Own

Write the missing numbers.

I. Put 20 sandwiches equally onto 5 trays.

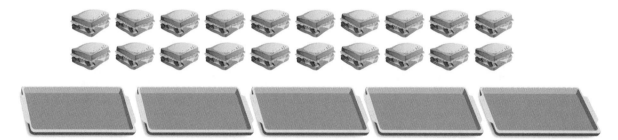

20 ÷ 5 = _____

There are _____ sandwiches on each tray.

2.

5 groups of _____   _____ groups of 5

5 × _____ = 10   _____ × 5 = 10

10 ÷ 5 = _____   10 ÷ 5 = _____

3.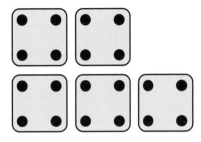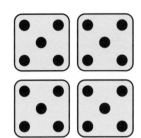

5 groups of _____

$20 \div 5 =$ _____

_____ groups of 5

$20 \div 5 =$ _____

Think!

4. USE MATH LANGUAGE Divide 20 stars into equal groups. Write down different ways. Write a division equation and a multiplication equation to show each way.

3K Divide by 10

A bracelet has 10 beads. How many similar bracelets can you make with 90 beads?

Learn

90 ÷ 10 = _____

I can make _____ bracelets.

Learn Together

1. There are 80 light bulbs.
   Put the light bulbs into groups of 10.

80 ÷ 10 = _____

_____ × 10 = 80

There are _____ groups of light bulbs.

Write the missing numbers.

2.
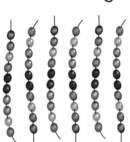

_____ groups of 10

_____ × 10 = 60

60 ÷ 10 = _____

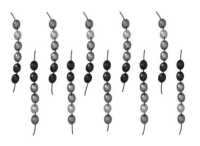

10 groups of _____

10 × _____ = 60

60 ÷ 10 = _____

3.

10 × _____ = 10

10 ÷ 10 = _____

_____ × 10 = 10

10 ÷ 10 = _____

Practice On Your Own

Write the missing numbers.

1. Put 70 erasers equally into 10 packs.

$70 \div 10 =$ _____

There are _____ erasers in each pack.

2.

 groups of 10

_____ × 10 = 40

$40 \div 10 =$ _____

10 groups of _____

$10 \times$ _____ $= 40$

$40 \div 10 =$ _____

3.

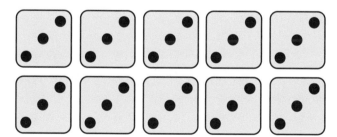

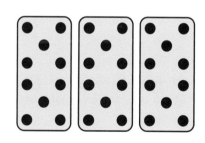

10 groups of _____

$30 \div 10 =$ _____

_____ groups of 10

$30 \div 10 =$ _____

Think!

4. USE STRUCTURE Brady has 30 strawberries.

   (a) He divides the strawberries into groups of 10.

   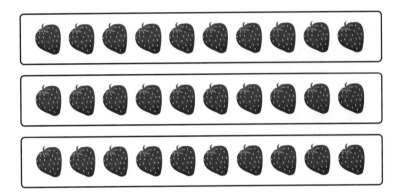

   30 ÷ 10 = _____

   (b) Then he divides the strawberries into groups of 5.

   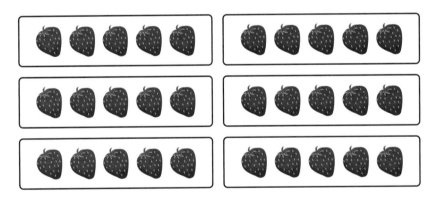

   30 ÷ 5 = _____

   (c) How are 30 ÷ 10 and 30 ÷ 5 related? Explain your answer.

3L Divide by 3

Arrange 30 books equally onto 3 shelves. How many books are there on each shelf? How can you find the answer?

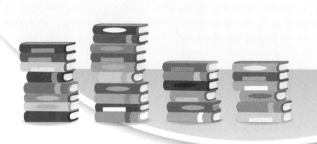

Learn

$30 \div 3 =$ _____

There are _____ books on each shelf.

Learn Together

1. Put 12 eggs equally into 3 baskets.

$12 \div 3 =$ _____

$3 \times 4 = 12$

There are _____ eggs in each basket.

Write the missing numbers.

2.

_____ groups of 3   3 groups of _____

_____ × 3 = 12   3 × _____ = 12

12 ÷ 3 = _____   12 ÷ 3 = _____

3.

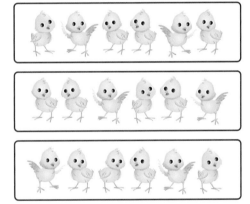

3 × _____ = 18   18 ÷ 3 = _____

4.   (a)

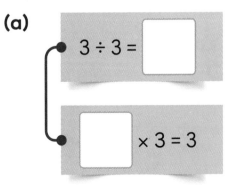

3 ÷ 3 = ☐

☐ × 3 = 3

(b)

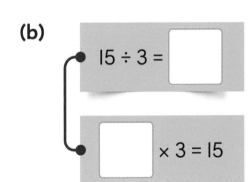

15 ÷ 3 = ☐

☐ × 3 = 15

Activity!

USE TOOLS AND MODEL Use 15 to make triangles. Draw the triangles.

Then write multiplication and division equations to show your work.

Practice On Your Own

Write the missing numbers.

I. Put 27 strawberries equally onto 3 plates.

27 ÷ 3 = _____

There are _____ strawberries on each plate.

2.

_____ groups of 3   _____ groups of _____

_____ × 3 = 15   _____ × _____ = 15

15 ÷ 3 = _____   15 ÷ _____ = _____

3. (a)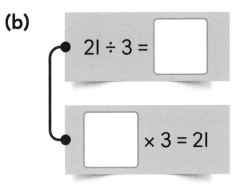

6 ÷ 3 = ☐

☐ × 3 = 6

(b)

21 ÷ 3 = ☐

☐ × 3 = 21

Think!

4. PERSEVERE In the diagrams below, each color stands for a number. When a number is multiplied by the number next to it, the answer is the number directly above the two numbers.

Write the missing numbers.

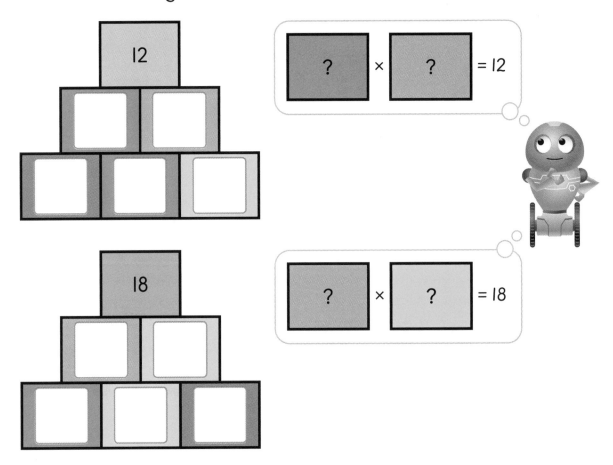

? × ? = 12

? × ? = 18

3M Divide by 4

Aimee wants to put 4 flowers in each vase. How many vases does she need?

I have 12 flowers.

Learn

$12 \div 4 =$ _____

She needs _____ vases.

Activity!

USE TOOLS AND MODEL Put 16 🎥 equally into 4 bags. Then write a division equation. Draw to show your work.

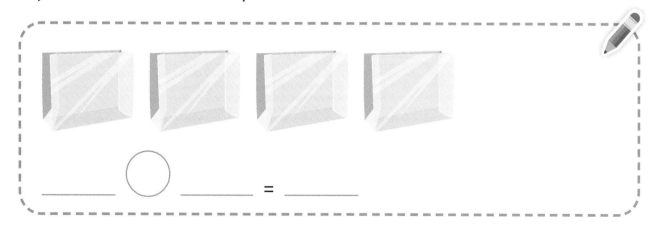

_____ ◯ _____ = _____

Learn Together

I. Put 20 roses equally into 4 vases.

$20 \div 4 =$ _____

 $4 \times 5 = 20$

There are _____ roses in each vase.

Write the missing numbers.

2.

_____ groups of 4 _____ groups of _____

_____ × 4 = 8 _____ × _____ = 8

$8 \div 4 =$ _____ $8 \div$ _____ = _____

3.

$32 \div 4 =$ ⬜ —— ⬜ $\times 4 = 32$

Practice On Your Own

Write the missing numbers.

I.   Put 40 beads equally onto 4 strings to make bracelets.

$40 \div 4 =$ _____

There are _____ beads on each bracelet.

2.

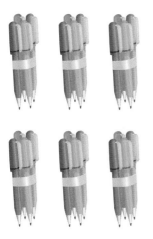   

_____ groups of 4   4 groups of _____

_____ × 4 = 24   4 × _____ = 24

$24 \div 4 =$ _____ $24 \div 4 =$ _____

3.

$4 \times$ _____ $= 28$ $28 \div 4 =$ _____

4.

$36 \div 4 =$ [ ] ●━━━● [ ] $\times 4 = 36$

Think!

5. REASON Can you put 19 teddy bears equally into 4 boxes? Explain your answer.

3N Word Problems

5 children share 30 strawberries equally. How many strawberries will each child get?

Learn

Will each child get the same number of strawberries? How do I know?

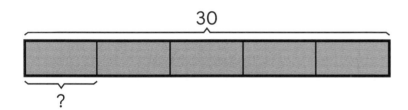

30 ÷ _____ = _____

Each child will get _____ strawberries.

Check:

_____ × _____ = _____

The answer is correct.

Learn Together

1. There are 10 chairs in a room. The chairs are arranged into 2 equal rows. How many chairs are there in each row?

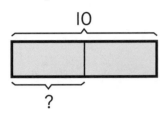

   $10 \div 2 =$ _____

   There are _____ chairs in each row.

2. Kiri has 24 toy cars. He packs the toy cars equally into 3 boxes. How many toy cars are there in each box?

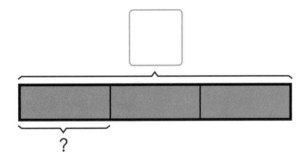

   _____ $\bigcirc$ _____ = _____

   There are _____ toy cars in each box.

3. Mrs. Johnson bakes 40 muffins. She puts the muffins equally onto 5 plates. How many muffins are there on each plate?

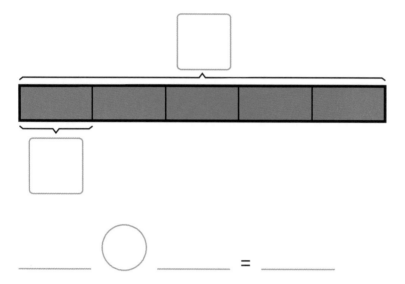

_____ _____ = _____

There are _____ muffins on each plate.

Practice On Your Own

Solve. Show your work.

1. There are 12 jars of honey. Emma puts the jars equally into 2 boxes. How many jars of honey are there in each box?

There are _____ jars of honey in each box.

2. Gavin has 28 stickers. He puts the stickers equally in 4 rows. How many stickers are there in each row?

There are _____ stickers in each row.

3. A store owner sells 10 toy robots. He receives $100 in all. How much does each toy robot cost?

Each toy robot costs $_____.

Mr. Brown plants 20 seeds in his garden.
He puts 5 seeds in each row.
How many rows of seeds are there?

Learn

What do I know? What do I have to find?
Do I multiply or divide?

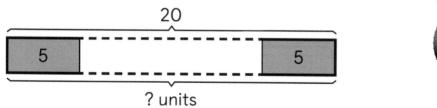

20 ÷ 5 = _____

There are _____ rows of seeds.

Check:

_____ × 5 = _____

The answer is correct.

Learn Together

1. Mrs. King folds 35 towels into stacks of 5. How many stacks of towels are there?

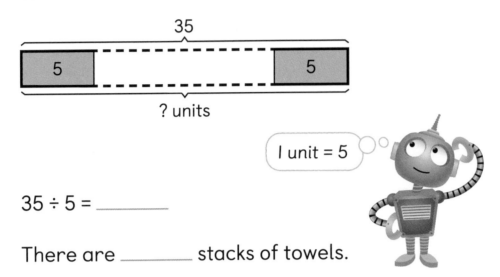

$35 \div 5 =$ _____

There are _____ stacks of towels.

2. A chef buys 40 pounds of potatoes. Each bag holds 10 pounds of potatoes. How many bags of potatoes does he buy?

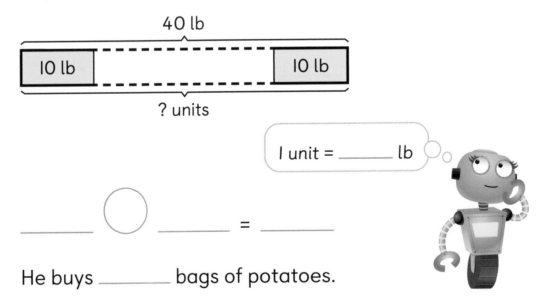

_____ ◯ _____ = _____

He buys _____ bags of potatoes.

Practice On Your Own 📝

Solve. Show your work.

1. Marcus sews 3 buttons on each shirt. He sews 21 buttons in all. How many shirts does he sew buttons on?

    He sews buttons on _____ shirts.

2. John puts 32 cookies equally into 4 jars. How many cookies are there in each jar?

    There are _____ cookies in each jar.

3. Avery has 6 vases. She puts 5 flowers into each vase. How many flowers are there in all?

    There are _____ flowers in all.

4. There are 6 children at a party. Each child gets 3 balloons. How many balloons do the children get in all?

The children get _____ balloons in all.

Think!

5. REASON Victor harvests 36 tomatoes and packs them equally into bags of 4. He says that he needs 8 bags in all. Do you agree with him? Explain your answer.

Performance Task

Mr. Rogers sells bottles of juice in his store.

He has 40 bottles of juice. He sells each bottle for $3.

I. **(a)** MODEL He arranges the bottles into 4 equal rows.
Draw a picture to show the arrangement.

(b) How many bottles of juice are there in each row?

There are _____ bottles of juice in each row.

(c) MODEL AND REASON Draw to show another way to arrange
the bottles in equal rows. Explain and write the related
multiplication equation.

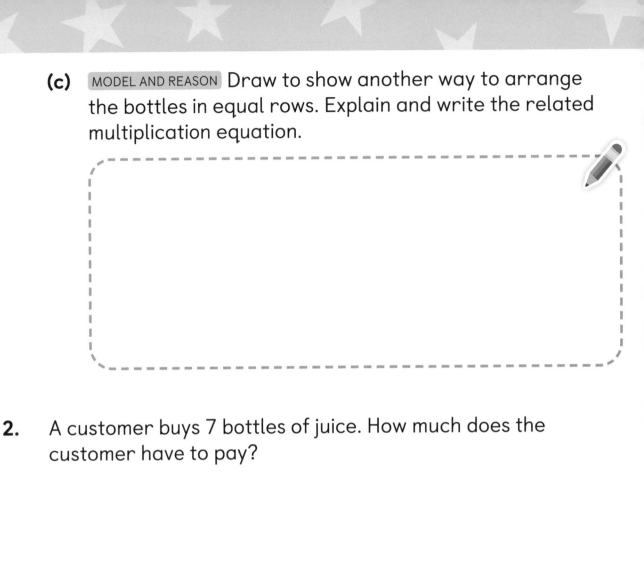

2. A customer buys 7 bottles of juice. How much does the
customer have to pay?

The customer has to pay $_____.

3. MODEL Plan a party for your friends. You have $24. Each
friend will get at least 2 bottles of juice at the party. How
many friends can you invite? How many bottles do you need
to buy?

How Did I Do?

My work is accurate.
I explain my thinking clearly.
I can apply my thinking in word problems.
I can justify why my strategy fits the situation.

I am mostly accurate.
I explain my thinking clearly.
I can apply my thinking to calculations.
I can use multiple strategies.

I show little work.
I do not explain my thinking clearly.
I am struggling with word problems.
I can only think of one way to solve a problem.

My Teacher's Words

Project Work

Telling time

Have you wondered why there are 60 minutes in an hour, not 100 or any other number? Why are there 12 hours on an analog clock, not 10, 15, or 20? We are using a base-60 system that originated around 3,000 BC. This system was widely used by the ancient Babylonians. 60 is the smallest number that can be divided by the first six counting numbers: 1, 2, 3, 4, 5, 6. The number 60 can also be divided by 10, 12, 15, 20, and 30, making it a very flexible number.

Task

1. Use the internet to learn more about the base-60 (sexagesimal) numeral system and how we use it in our daily lives.

2. Create your own time system using the multiplication facts you have learned.

3. Use your time system to create a schedule. Show the various activities you do at different times of the day.

4. Show the start times, end times, and duration of each activity in your schedule.

5. Put up each group's work onto a wall. Share your work.

Chapter Practice

I. There are 4 muffins in each box.
How many muffins are there in 6 boxes?

(A) 10

(B) 24

(C) 32

(D) 46

2. Which of the following is **not** correct?

(A) $3 \times 7 = 7 \times 3$

(B) $7 \times 0 = 7$

(C) $7 \times 3 = 21$

(D) $7 + 7 + 7 = 21$

3. Multiply.

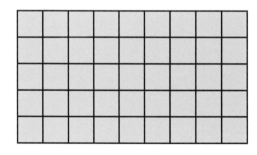
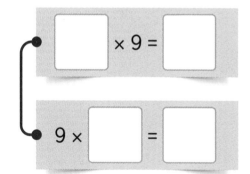

$\boxed{} \times 9 = \boxed{}$

$9 \times \boxed{} = \boxed{}$

4. How much money is there?

_____ × _____ = _____

There is $_____ .

5.

$5 \times 3 =$ _____ $6 \times 3 =$ _____ + _____

                                                    $=$ _____

6.

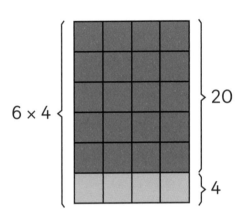

$5 \times 4 =$ _____

$1 \times 4 =$ _____

$6 \times 4 =$ _____ + _____

$=$ _____

7. **(a)**

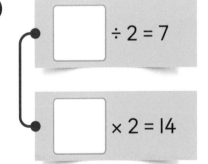

☐ $\div 2 = 7$

☐ $\times 2 = 14$

(b)

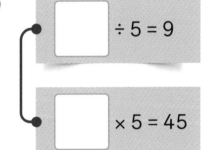

☐ $\div 5 = 9$

☐ $\times 5 = 45$

Solve. Show your work.

8. Mr. Flores arranges some chairs for a meeting. He arranges 5 rows of chairs. Each row has 7 chairs. How many chairs are there in all?

There are _____ chairs in all.

9. Tiana has 90 building blocks. She wants to put 10 building blocks into each bag. How many bags does she need?

She needs _____ bags.

10. REASON AND USE STRUCTURE What is the missing number in the multiplication equation? Explain your answer.

$$4 \times 3 = ? \times 4$$

II. PERSEVERE What number does each letter stand for?

a = _____   b = _____   c = _____

d = _____   e = _____   f = _____

g = _____   h = _____

Solve! Heuristics: Look for a Pattern

Sophia is hanging pictures on a string. She uses 2 clips to hang a picture, 3 clips to hang 2 pictures, 4 clips to hang 3 pictures, and so on. How many clips will she need to hang 15 pictures?

| Step 1 | **Understand** | How many clips does Sophia use for 1 picture? 2 pictures? 3 pictures? |

| Step 2 | **Plan** | I need to **look for a pattern** between the number of pictures and the number of clips. |

| Step 3 | **Do** |

Make a table and observe the pattern.

Number of pictures	1	2	3	15
Number of clips	2	3	4	?

+ 1   + 1

Sophia uses 2 clips to hang 1 picture.
She will need 1 more clip to hang each additional picture.

2 + 14 = 16

Sophia will need 16 clips to hang 15 pictures.

| Step 4 | **Look Back** |

Check that the answer makes sense.

Is there another way to solve the problem?

Solve.

1.   Felipe makes some hexagons using craft sticks.

How many craft sticks does he need to make 10 hexagons?

2.   A square table can seat 4 people. Joining 2 square tables side by side can seat 6 people.

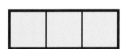

How many people can be seated at 3 tables?
How many tables are needed for 20 people?

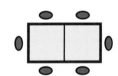

4 MULTIPLICATION AND DIVISION OF 6, 7, 8, AND 9

Multiplication facts you have learned

×	1	2	3	4	5	6	7	8	9	10
1	1	2	3	4	5	6	7	8	9	10
2	2	4	6	8	10	12	14	16	18	20
3	3	6	9	12	15	18	21	24	27	30
4	4	8	12	16	20	24	28	32	36	40
5	5	10	15	20	25	30	35	40	45	50
6	6	12	18	24	30					60
7	7	14	21	28	35					70
8	8	16	24	32	40					80
9	9	18	27	36	45					90
10	10	20	30	40	50	60	70	80	90	100

We have 9 friends. We have to give each friend 6 stickers. How many stickers do we need in all?

How do we use the chart to help us?

How do you use patterns in the chart to help you find the remaining 16 facts?

Recall

1. Write the missing numbers.

(a)

$4 \times 6 =$ _____

$24 \div 4 =$ _____

(b)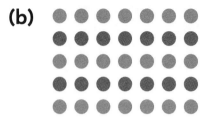

$5 \times 7 =$ _____

$35 \div 5 =$ _____

2. Write a multiplication equation and a division equation.

_____ ◯ _____ = _____

_____ ◯ _____ = _____

3. REASON Match each bar model to a word problem.

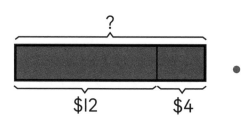

•

• Anya has $12. She spends $4. How much money does she have left?

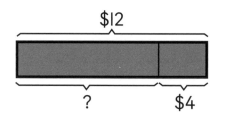

•

• Isabel has $4 less than Joseph. Isabel has $12. How much money does Joseph have?

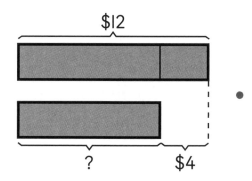

•

• Jade and her three sisters have $3 each. How much money do they have in all?

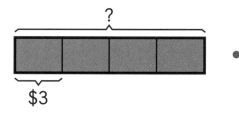

•

• Layla has $12. Her father gives her another $4. How much money does she have now?

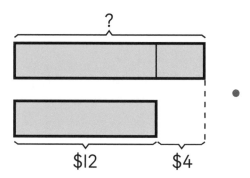

•

• Caleb has $12. He has $4 more than Chloe. How much money does Chloe have?

4. Write the related multiplication and division equations using the numbers given.

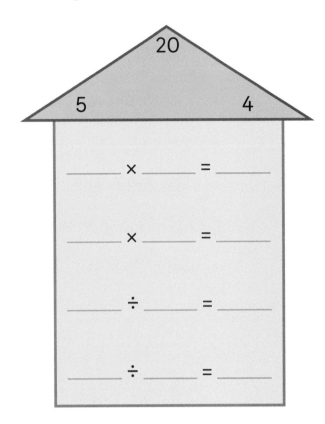

_____ × _____ = _____

_____ × _____ = _____

_____ ÷ _____ = _____

_____ ÷ _____ = _____

_____ × _____ = _____

_____ × _____ = _____

_____ ÷ _____ = _____

_____ ÷ _____ = _____

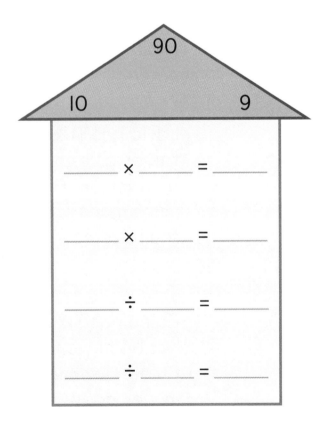

_____ × _____ = _____

_____ × _____ = _____

_____ ÷ _____ = _____

_____ ÷ _____ = _____

I can...

☐ multiply and divide by 2, 3, 4, 5, and 10.

☐ understand part-whole and comparison models.

☐ write related multiplication and division facts.

4A Multiply and Divide by 6

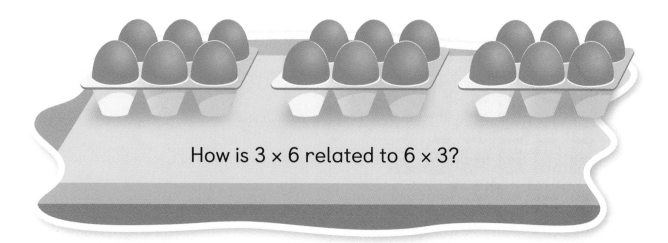

How is 3 × 6 related to 6 × 3?

Learn

3 sixes is equal to 6 threes.

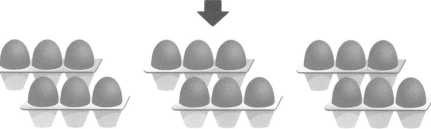

3 × 6 = 6 + 6 + 6
     = 18

6 × 3 = 3 + 3 + 3 + 3 + 3 + 3
     = 18

3 × 6 = 6 × 3

The **product** of 3 and 6 is 18.

 You can also find 3 × 6 from 3 × 5. How?

Learn Together

I. Multiply.

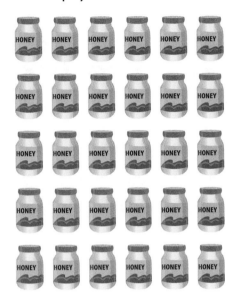

$5 \times 6 = 6 \times 5$

$= \underline{\hspace{2cm}}$

2. Multiply 6 by 6.

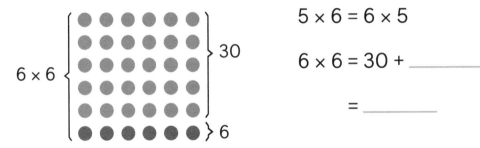

$5 \times 6 = 6 \times 5$

$6 \times 6 = 30 + \underline{\hspace{2cm}}$

$= \underline{\hspace{2cm}}$

3. Find the product of 9 and 6.

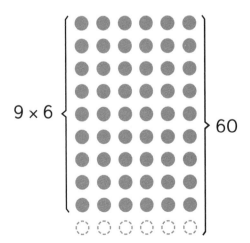

$10 \times 6 = 60$

$9 \times 6 = 60 - \underline{\hspace{2cm}}$

$= \underline{\hspace{2cm}}$

Write the missing numbers.

4.

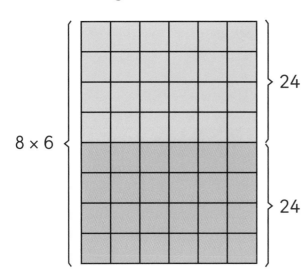

8 × 6

24

24

8 × 6 = Double 24

4 × 6 = _____

8 × 6 = _____

How would you find
6 × 6 using 3 × 6?

5.

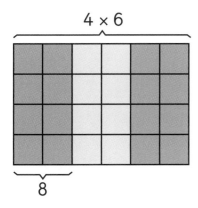

4 × 6

8

4 × 6 = _____ + _____ + _____

= _____

Add 4 × 2 three times.

4 × 6

12

4 × 6 = _____ + _____

= _____

Add 4 × 3 two times.

Activity!

USE STRUCTURE Discuss with your classmate and write down different ways to find 8 × 6.

Practice On Your Own

Write the missing numbers.

1.

6 × 2 = _____

2 × 6 = _____

2.

30

12

5 × 6 = _____

2 × 6 = _____

7 × 6 = _____ + _____

= _____

3.

12

2 × 6 = _____

6 × 6 = _____ + _____ + _____

= _____

4.

0 × 6 = _____	6 × 0 = _____
1 × 6 = _____	6 × 1 = _____
2 × 6 = _____	6 × 2 = _____
3 × 6 = _____	6 × _____ = _____
4 × 6 = _____	6 × _____ = _____
5 × 6 = _____	6 × _____ = _____
6 × 6 = _____	6 × _____ = _____
7 × 6 = _____	6 × _____ = _____
8 × 6 = _____	6 × _____ = _____
9 × 6 = _____	6 × _____ = _____
10 × 6 = _____	6 × _____ = _____

5 + 1

10 + 2

15 + 3

20 + 4

25 + 5

30 + 6

35 + 7

40 + 8

45 + 9

50 + 10

5.   Color rows of 6. Then write the multiplication fact.

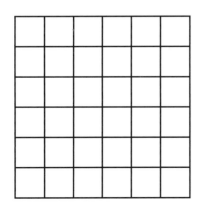

? × 6 = ?

_____ × _____ = _____

Think!

6. LOOK FOR PATTERNS Look at the multiplication chart.

(a) Write the missing numbers.

×	1	2	3	4	5	6	7	8	9	10
1	1	2	3	4	5		7	8	9	10
2	2	4	6	8	10		14	16	18	20
3	3	6	9	12	15		21	24	27	30
4	4	8	12	16	20		28	32	36	40
5	5	10	15	20	25		35	40	45	50
6										
7	7	14	21	28	35		49	56	63	70
8	8	16	24	32	40		56	64	72	80
9	9	18	27	36	45		63	72	81	90
10	10	20	30	40	50		70	80	90	100

(b) Look at the multiplication facts of 3 and 6 in the chart. What patterns do you see?

(c) If 3 × 11 = 33, what is 6 × 11? Explain your answer.

How many hexagons can the children make with 24 craft sticks?

Learn

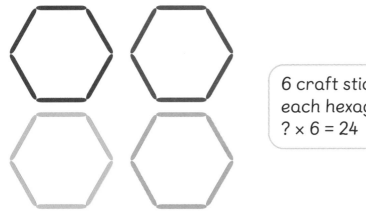

6 craft sticks for each hexagon.
? × 6 = 24

24 ÷ 6 = 4

The children can make 4 hexagons.

When we divide 24 by 6, the **quotient** is 4.

Learn Together

Write the missing numbers.

1. 30 comic books are shared equally among 6 classes.
    How many comic books does each class get?

30 ÷ 6 = _____

6 × _____ = 30

Each class gets _____ comic books.

2.

_____ groups of 6   6 groups of _____

_____ × 6 = 30   6 × _____ = 30

30 ÷ 6 = _____   30 ÷ 6 = _____

3.

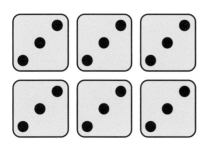 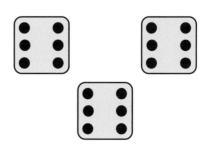

$6 \times$ _____ $= 18$ _____ $\times 6 = 18$

$18 \div 6 =$ _____ $18 \div 3 =$ _____

4. **(a)**

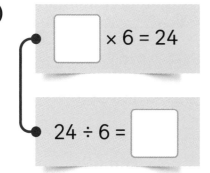

$\boxed{} \times 6 = 24$

$24 \div 6 = \boxed{}$

(b)

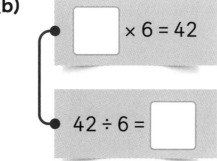

$\boxed{} \times 6 = 42$

$42 \div 6 = \boxed{}$

5. Find the quotient when 54 is divided by 6.

$54 \div 6 =$ _____

Practice On Your Own

Write the missing numbers.

1. There are 12 apples. Each crate holds 6 apples. How many crates are needed?

$12 \div 6 =$ _____

_____ crates are needed.

2.

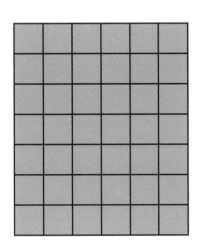

_____ × 6 = 24

24 ÷ 6 = _____

6 × _____ = 24

24 ÷ 6 = _____

3.

_____ × 6 = 42

42 ÷ 6 = _____

4. **(a)**

36 ÷ 6 = ☐

☐ × 6 = 36

(b)

48 ÷ 6 = ☐

☐ × 6 = 48

> I pack 6 rolls into each box.

Mr. Jones bakes 60 rolls.
He packs 6 rolls into each empty box.
How many boxes of rolls are there?

Learn

Step 1 **Draw a bar model to help you understand the problem.**

> What do I know?
> What do I have to find?
> Do I multiply or divide?

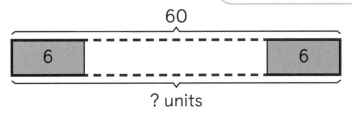

Step 2 **Solve.**

$60 \div 6 = $ _____

There are _____ boxes of rolls.

Step 3 **Check.**
$10 \times 6 = 60$
The answer is correct.

Learn Together

1. There are 6 packs of juice boxes. Each pack contains 10 juice boxes. How many juice boxes are there in all?

    6 groups of 10

    6 × 10 = _____

    There are _____ juice boxes in all.

2. Mrs. Beck puts 12 eggs equally into some empty bowls. There are 6 eggs in each bowl. How many bowls of eggs does she have?

    _____ × 6 = 12

    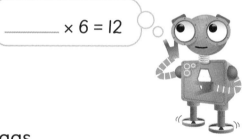

    12 ÷ 6 = _____

    She has _____ bowls of eggs.

3. Sticky notes are sold in sets of 6. Mrs. Romero has 18 students in her class. How many sets of sticky notes would she need to have enough for each student?

    18 ÷ 6 = _____

    She would need _____ sets.

4. Mr. James buys 4 packs of paper towels. Each pack has 6 rolls. How many rolls of paper towels does he buy?

_____ 〇 _____ = _____

He buys _____ rolls of paper towels.

Practice On Your Own

Solve. Show your work.

1. A bargain store sells T-shirts for a back-to-school sale. T-shirts cost $48 for a pack of 6. How much does each T-shirt cost?

Each T-shirt costs $_____.

2. In the store, the T-shirts are stacked according to color. There are 54 shirts in 6 equal stacks. How many T-shirts in each color are there?

There are _____ T-shirts in each color.

3. Margo draws a house using 6 lines. How many lines would she need to draw 3 of these houses?

She would need to draw _____ lines.

4. Butterflies taste with their feet. Butterflies have 6 legs each.

Write the missing numbers.

Number of butterflies	4			
Total number of legs		30	36	42

4B Multiply and Divide by 7

There are 7 dots on the back of each ladybug.
What are the different ways to find 3 × 7?

Learn

3 groups of 7

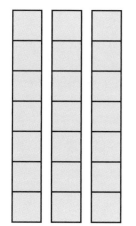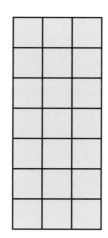

3 × 7 = 7 × 3

= _____

 How would you use
3 × 5 to find 3 × 7?

Learn Together

1. Multiply.

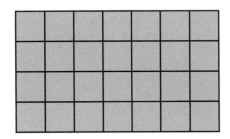

$7 \times 4 =$ _____

$4 \times 7 =$ _____

2. Multiply 6 by 7.

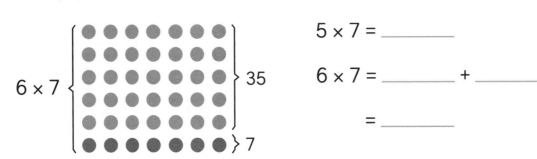

6×7 ⎰ ⎱ 35 ⎰ 7

$5 \times 7 =$ _____

$6 \times 7 =$ _____ + _____

$=$ _____

3. Find the product of 7 and 7.

7×7 ⎰ ⎱ 35 ⎰ 14

$5 \times 7 =$ _____

$2 \times 7 =$ _____

$7 \times 7 =$ _____ + _____

$=$ _____

Write the missing numbers.

4.

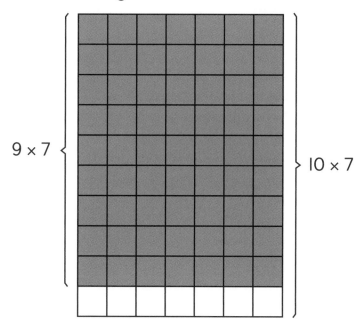

$10 \times 7 =$ _____

9×7

$=$ _____ $-$ _____

$=$ _____

5.

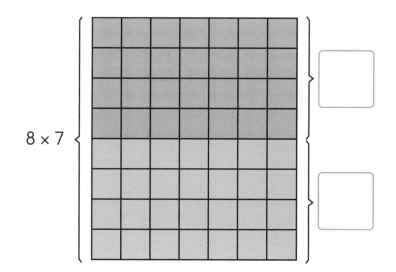

$4 \times 7 =$ _____

8×7

$=$ _____ $+$ _____

$=$ _____

Activity!

USE STRUCTURE Write down different ways to find 8×7. Share your answer with your classmate.

Practice On Your Own

Write the missing numbers.

1.

$7 \times 2 =$ _____

$2 \times 7 =$ _____

2.

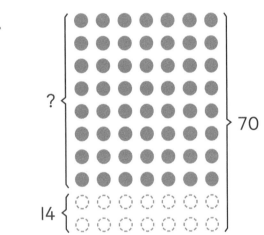

$10 \times 7 =$ _____

$2 \times 7 =$ _____

$8 \times 7 =$ _____ – _____

$=$ _____

3.

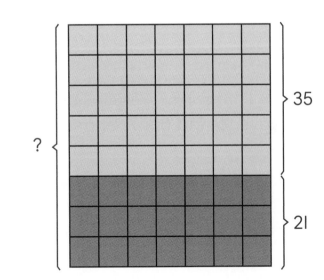

$5 \times 7 =$ _____

$3 \times 7 =$ _____

$8 \times 7 =$ _____ + _____

$=$ _____

4.

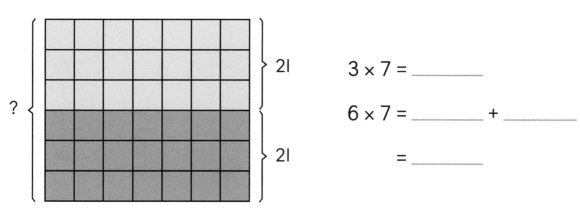

$3 \times 7 =$ _____

$6 \times 7 =$ _____ + _____

$=$ _____

5.

$0 \times 7 =$ _____	$7 \times 0 =$ _____
$1 \times 7 =$ _____	$7 \times 1 =$ _____
$2 \times 7 =$ _____	$7 \times 2 =$ _____
$3 \times 7 =$ _____	$7 \times$ _____ $=$ _____
$4 \times 7 =$ _____	$7 \times$ _____ $=$ _____
$5 \times 7 =$ _____	$7 \times$ _____ $=$ _____
$6 \times 7 =$ _____	$7 \times$ _____ $=$ _____
$7 \times 7 =$ _____	$7 \times$ _____ $=$ _____
$8 \times 7 =$ _____	$7 \times$ _____ $=$ _____
$9 \times 7 =$ _____	$7 \times$ _____ $=$ _____
$10 \times 7 =$ _____	$7 \times$ _____ $=$ _____

Think!

6. LOOK FOR PATTERNS Look at the multiplication chart.

(a) Write the missing numbers.

×	1	2	3	4	5	6	7	8	9	10
1	1	2	3	4	5	6		8	9	10
2	2	4	6	8	10	12		16	18	20
3	3	6	9	12	15	18		24	27	30
4	4	8	12	16	20	24		32	36	40
5	5	10	15	20	25	30		40	45	50
6	6	12	18	24	30	36		48	54	60
7										
8	8	16	24	32	40	48		64	72	80
9	9	18	27	36	45	54		72	81	90
10	10	20	30	40	50	60		80	90	100

(b) Look at the multiplication facts of 2, 5, and 7 in the chart. What pattern do you see?

How many weeks are there in 28 days?

Learn

28 ÷ 7 = _____

There are _____ weeks.

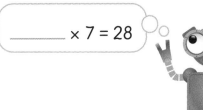

_____ × 7 = 28

Learn Together

I. 21 flowers are shared equally among some children.
Each child gets 7 flowers.
How many children are there?

7 × _____ = 21

21 ÷ 7 = _____

There are _____ children.

Write the missing numbers.

2.

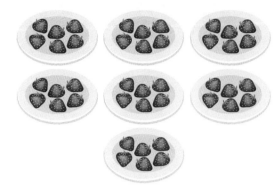

7 groups of _____

7 × _____ = 42

42 ÷ 7 = _____

_____ groups of 7

_____ × 7 = 42

42 ÷ 7 = _____

3.

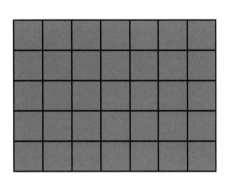

_____ × 7 = 35

35 ÷ 7 = _____

7 × _____ = 35

35 ÷ 5 = _____

4. **(a)**

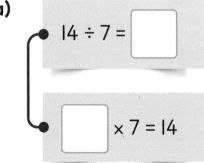

14 ÷ 7 = ☐

☐ × 7 = 14

(b)

49 ÷ 7 = ☐

☐ × 7 = 49

Practice On Your Own ✏️

Write the missing numbers.

1.

_____ × 7 = 21   7 × _____ = 21

21 ÷ 7 = _____   21 ÷ 7 = _____

2.

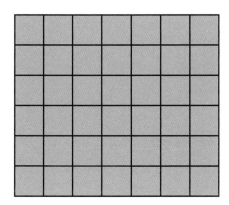

_____ × 7 = 42   7 × _____ = 42

42 ÷ 7 = _____   42 ÷ 6 = _____

3. **(a)**

$7 \div 7 = \boxed{}$

$\boxed{} \times 7 = 7$

(b)

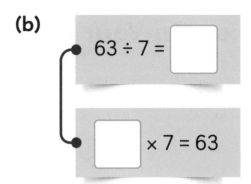

$63 \div 7 = \boxed{}$

$\boxed{} \times 7 = 63$

Think!

4. PERSEVERE In the diagram below, the number in each triangle is the product of three letters around it. What number does each letter stand for?

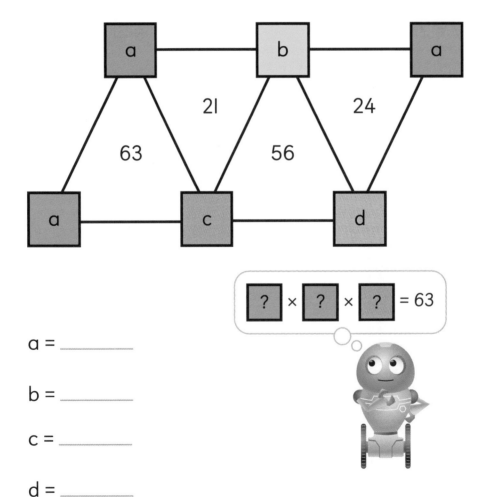

$\boxed{?} \times \boxed{?} \times \boxed{?} = 63$

a = _____

b = _____

c = _____

d = _____

7 children did jumping jacks.
They did 21 jumping jacks altogether.
Each child did the same number of jumping jacks.
How many jumping jacks did each child do?

Learn

What do I know?
What do I have to find?
Do I multiply or divide?

21

?

21 ÷ 7 = _____

Each child did _____ jumping jacks.

Check:

3 × 7 = _____

The answer is correct.

Learn Together

1. Jim earns $10 for each lawn he mows. He mows 7 lawns. How much does he earn from mowing the lawns?

    7 groups of 10

    $7 \times 10 =$ _____

    He earns $_____.

2. There are 14 apples in some bowls. Each bowl has 7 apples. How many bowls of apples are there?

    _____ ÷ _____ = _____

    There are _____ bowls of apples.

3. A box can hold 7 toy cars. How many toy cars can 4 boxes hold altogether?

    $4 \times 7 =$ _____

    The boxes can hold _____ toy cars altogether.

4. Bella wants to make 7 identical bracelets. She has 21 red beads and 28 blue beads.

  (a) How many red beads does each bracelet have?

  _____ ◯ _____ = _____

  Each bracelet has _____ red beads.

  (b) How many blue beads does each bracelet have?

  _____ ◯ _____ = _____

  Each bracelet has _____ blue beads.

Practice On Your Own 📝

Solve. Show your work.

1. Lily packs 7 pears into a bag. How many bags does she need for 14 pears?

  She needs _____ bags.

2. Kiara puts 56 tomatoes equally into 7 bags. How many tomatoes are there in each bag?

  There are _____ tomatoes in each bag.

3. A restaurant is open 6 days a week. It serves food 7 hours a day. How many hours is the restaurant open in a week?

The restaurant is open _____ hours in a week.

4. A fruit stand is open 7 days a week. It is open 8 hours a day. How many hours is the fruit stand open in a week?

The fruit stand is open _____ hours in a week.

5. A heptagon has 7 sides.

Write the missing numbers.

Number of heptagons	1		7		9
Number of sides	7	28		56	

4C Multiply and Divide by 8

How would you use 3 × 4
to find 3 × 8?

Learn

3 groups of 8

$3 \times 4 = 12$
$3 \times 8 = (3 \times 4) + (3 \times 4)$
$\qquad = 12 + 12$
$\qquad = 24$

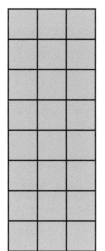  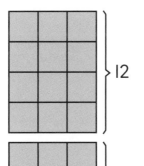 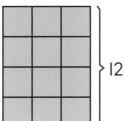

12

12

Learn Together

Write the missing numbers.

1.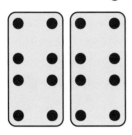

Double 8
8 + 8

$2 \times 8 =$ _____

2.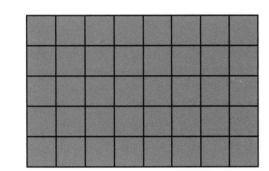

$5 \times 8 =$ _____

$8 \times 5 =$ _____

3.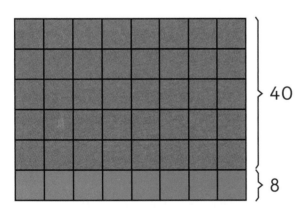

$5 \times 8 =$ _____

$6 \times 8 =$ _____

40

8

4.

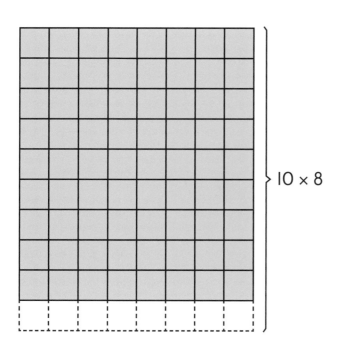

$10 \times 8 =$ _____

$9 \times 8 =$ _____

5.

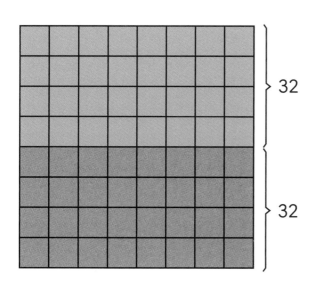

$4 \times 8 =$ _____

$8 \times 8 =$ _____

6.

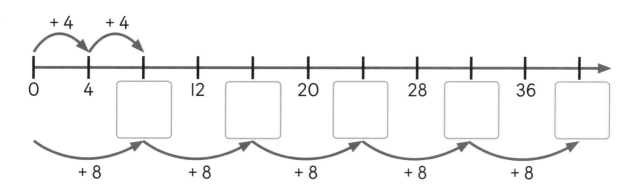

Practice On Your Own

Write the missing numbers.

I.

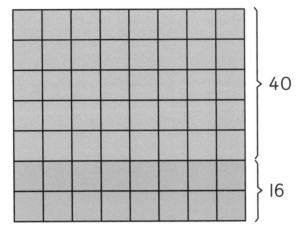

40

16

5 × 8 = _____

2 × 8 = _____

7 × 8 = _____

2.

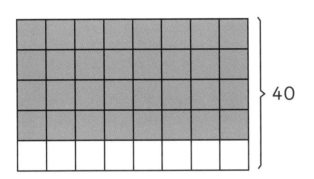

40

5 × 8 = _____

4 × 8 = _____

3.

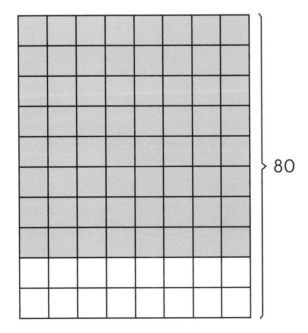

80

10 × 8 = _____

2 × 8 = _____

8 × 8 = _____

4.

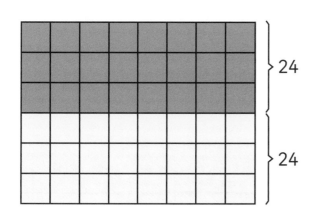

$3 \times 8 =$ _____

$6 \times 8 =$ _____

5.

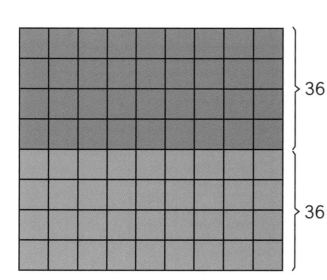

$9 \times 4 =$ _____

$9 \times 8 =$ _____

6.

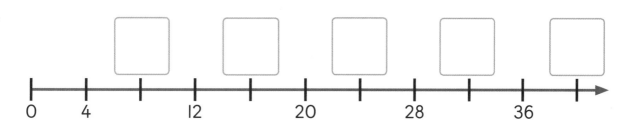

_____ $\times 4 = 40$

_____ $\times 8 = 40$

Think!

7. **LOOK FOR PATTERNS** Look at the multiplication chart.

(a) Write the missing numbers.

×	1	2	3	4	5	6	7	8	9	10
1	1	2	3	4	5	6	7		9	10
2	2	4	6	8	10	12	14		18	20
3	3	6	9	12	15	18	21		27	30
4	4	8	12	16	20	24	28		36	40
5	5	10	15	20	25	30	35		45	50
6	6	12	18	24	30	36	42		54	60
7	7	14	21	28	35	42	49		63	70
8										
9	9	18	27	36	45	54	63		81	90
10	10	20	30	40	50	60	70		90	100

(b) Look at the multiplication facts of 2, 4, and 8 in the chart. What patterns do you see?

Name: _____ Date: _____

Nicole builds a large cube using 8 small cubes.
How many large cubes can she build with 32 small cubes?

Learn

$32 \div 8 =$ _____

_____ × 8 = 32

She can build _____ large cubes.

Learn Together

I. Share 24 pencils equally among some children.
    Each child gets 8 pencils.
    How many children are there?

$24 \div 8 =$ _____

8 × _____ = 24

There are _____ children.

Write the missing numbers.

2.

_____ groups of 8   8 groups of _____

_____ × 8 = 16   8 × _____ = 16

16 ÷ 8 = _____   16 ÷ 8 = _____

3.

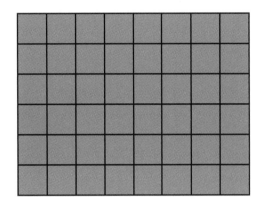

_____ × 8 = _____   8 × _____ = _____

_____ ÷ 8 = _____   _____ ÷ 6 = _____

4.

40 ÷ 8 = ☐ ●━━━● ☐ × 8 = 40

Activity!

MODEL 8 squares make a rectangle as shown.
Use 24 squares to make 3 rectangles.
Write a multiplication equation and a related
division equation to show the result.

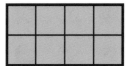

(dashed box for work)

Practice On Your Own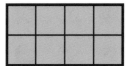

Write the missing numbers.

1. Mrs. Allen has 56 oranges. She wants to put 8 oranges into
    each bag. How many bags does she need?

$56 ÷ 8 =$ _____

She needs _____ bags.

2.

_____ × 8 = 40   8 × _____ = 40

40 ÷ 8 = _____   40 ÷ _____ = 8

3.

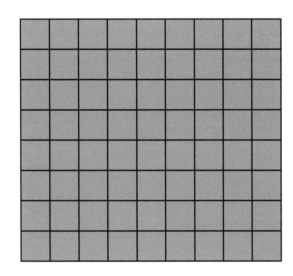

_____ × 8 = _____   _____ × 9 = _____

_____ ÷ 8 = _____   _____ ÷ 9 = _____

4.

64 ÷ 8 = ☐ ●━━━● ☐ × 8 = 64

Olive buys 8 stalks of flowers for her grandmother.
Each stalk costs $6.
How much does Olive pay for the flowers?

1 stalk for $6

Learn

What do I know?
What do I need to find?
Do I multiply or divide?

$6

?

8 × 6 = _____

Olive pays $_____ for the flowers.

Check:
8 is close to but less than 10.
10 stalks of flowers will cost $60.

$_____ is less than $60.
The answer is reasonable.

Learn Together

1. Max has 24 squares of fabric to make a quilt. He uses
    8 squares of fabric to sew each row of the quilt. How many
    rows does the quilt have?

    $24 \div 8 =$ _____

    _____ $\times 8 = 24$

    The quilt has _____ rows.

2. Faith makes 8 equal sets of trading cards. She has 40 football
    cards and 16 baseball cards. How many of each type of cards
    are there in each set?

    Number of football cards:

    $40 \div 8 =$ _____

    Number of baseball cards:

    $16 \div 8 =$ _____

    There are _____ football cards and _____ baseball cards
    in each set.

3. Mr. Williams sells 80 action figures in his store. The action figures are sold in boxes of 8. How many boxes of action figures are there?

_____ ◯ _____ = _____

There are _____ boxes of action figures.

4. Mrs. Fox buys 8 sets of building blocks for $72. Each set costs the same. What is the cost of each set?

_____ ◯ _____ = _____

The cost of each set is $_____.

Practice On Your Own

Solve. Show your work.

1. There are 6 players on a volleyball team. How many players are there on 8 teams?

There are _____ players on 8 teams.

2. 56 students sign up to play indoor soccer.
The students form 8 soccer teams.
How many students are there on each team?

There are _____ students on each team.

3. There are 72 baseball players at a competition.
There are 8 teams. How many players are there
on each team?

There are _____ players on each team.

4. There are 5 players on each basketball team.
There are 8 teams taking part in a tournament.
How many players are there altogether?

There are _____ players altogether.

4D Multiply and Divide by 9

9 triangle blocks make a large triangle as shown. How many triangle blocks are needed to make 3 triangles?

Learn

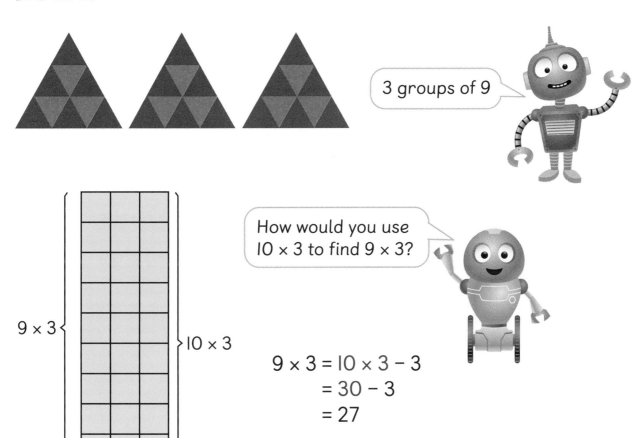

3 groups of 9

How would you use 10×3 to find 9×3?

$$9 \times 3 = 10 \times 3 - 3$$
$$= 30 - 3$$
$$= 27$$

Learn Together

Write the missing numbers.

1.

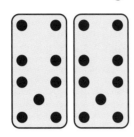 

$2 \times 9 =$ _____

2.

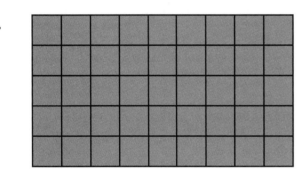

$5 \times 9 =$ _____

$9 \times 5 =$ _____

3.

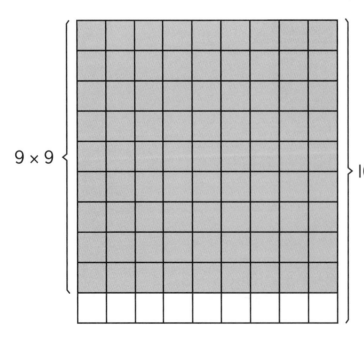

$10 \times 9 =$ _____

$9 \times 9 =$ _____

4.

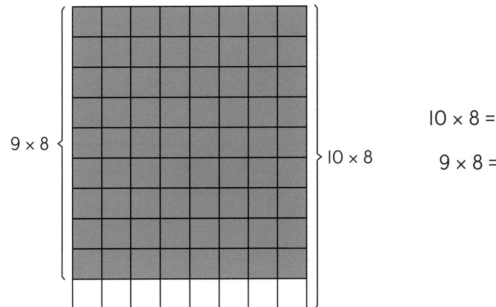

9×8 {

} 10×8

$10 \times 8 =$ _____

$9 \times 8 =$ _____

Activity!

USE STRUCTURE Use your fingers to show how to multiply by 9.

2 tens   7 ones   3 tens   6 ones

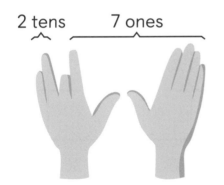

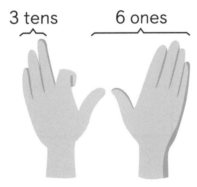

$3 \times 9 = 27$ $4 \times 9 = 36$

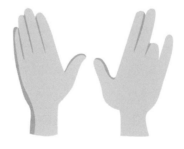

$7 \times 9 =$ _____ $9 \times 9 =$ _____

How do you show 2×9, 5×9, 6×9, and 8×9?
Explain why it works to your classmate.

Practice On Your Own

1. **(a)** Write the missing numbers.

×	1	2	3	4	5	6	7	8	9	10
1	1	2	3	4	5	6	7	8		10
2	2	4	6	8	10	12	14	16		20
3	3	6	9	12	15	18	21	24		30
4	4	8	12	16	20	24	28	32		40
5	5	10	15	20	25	30	35	40		50
6	6	12	18	24	30	36	42	48		60
7	7	14	21	28	35	42	49	56		70
8	8	16	24	32	40	48	56	64		80
9										
10	10	20	30	40	50	60	70	80		100

(b) Add the two digits of any fact of 9. What pattern do you see?

(c) What do you notice about the ones digits of the facts of 9?

Mr. Evans uses 9 oranges to make a jug of orange juice. How many jugs of juice can he make with 54 oranges?

Learn

$54 \div 9 =$ _____

_____ $\times\ 9 = 54$

He can make _____ jugs of juice.

Learn Together

I. Andrew uses 36 pieces of modeling clay to make 9 identical rabbit models. How many pieces of modeling clay does he use to make each rabbit model?

$36 \div 9 =$ _____

$9 \times$ _____ $= 36$

He uses _____ pieces of modeling clay to make each rabbit model.

Write the missing numbers.

2.

 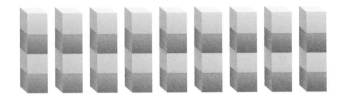

_____ groups of 9   9 groups of _____

_____ × 9 = 36   9 × _____ = 36

36 ÷ 9 = _____   36 ÷ 9 = _____

3.

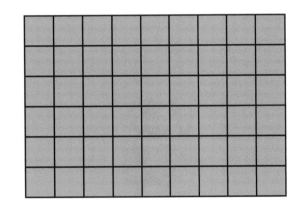

_____ × 9 = _____   _____ × _____ = _____

_____ ÷ 9 = _____   _____ ÷ _____ = _____

4. **(a)**

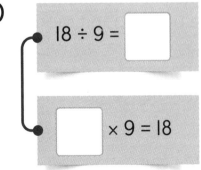

18 ÷ 9 = ☐

☐ × 9 = 18

(b)

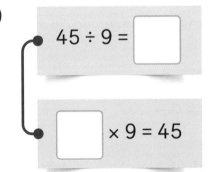

45 ÷ 9 = ☐

☐ × 9 = 45

Practice On Your Own

Write the missing numbers.

1. There are 63 balloons. 9 balloons are tied in a bunch.
How many bunches of balloons are there?

$63 \div 9 =$ _____

There are _____ bunches of balloons.

2.

_____ $\times 9 = 45$ $9 \times$ _____ $= 45$

$45 \div 9 =$ _____ $45 \div$ _____ $= 9$

3.

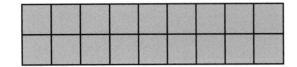

_____ × _____ = _____   _____ × _____ = _____

_____ ÷ _____ = _____   _____ ÷ _____ = _____

4. **(a)**

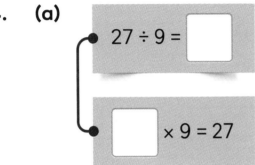

$27 ÷ 9 = \boxed{}$

$\boxed{} × 9 = 27$

(b)

$81 ÷ 9 = \boxed{}$

$\boxed{} × 9 = 81$

Think!

5. REASON Is $0 ÷ 9 = 9$? Explain using multiplication.

Caroline has $27.
It costs $9 an hour to rock climb.
How many hours can she rock climb?

Climbing for Children

$9 an hour
Harness and Helmet Included

Learn

What do I know?
What do I have to find?
Do I multiply or divide?

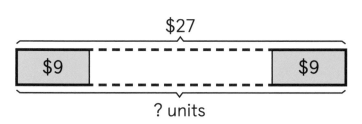

$27

| $9 | | $9 |

? units

27 ÷ 9 = _____

She can rock climb for _____ hours.

Check:

_____ × 9 = _____

The answer is correct.

Learn Together

1. Aika and 8 friends go ice-skating. Each admission costs $7. How much do they pay for admission?

    9 groups of 7

    $9 \times 7 =$ _____

    They pay $_____ for admission.

2. 9 boys buy a bucket of popcorn each at the movies. They pay $54 altogether. What is the cost of each bucket of popcorn?

    $9 \times$ _____ $= 54$

    $54 \div 9 =$ _____

    The cost of each bucket of popcorn is $_____.

3. Lola cuts 45 inches of tape into 9 equal pieces. How long is each piece of tape?

    _____ ⬡ _____ = _____

    Each piece of tape is _____ inches long.

4. Mr. Reed sells jelly at $9 for each jar. He collects $81 from the sale of the jelly. How many jars of jelly does he sell?

_____ ◯ _____ = _____   _____ × 9 = 81

He sells _____ jars of jelly.

5. Mr. Reed displays the jars on a cabinet with 6 shelves. There are 9 full jars of jelly and an empty jar on each shelf. How many full jars are there?

_____ ◯ _____ = _____

There are _____ full jars.

Discuss with your classmate how you can find the answer in another way.

Practice On Your Own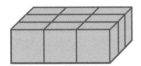

Solve. Show your work.

1. Brandon uses 9 cubes to make a layer as shown.
How many cubes does he need to build 5 layers?

He needs _____ cubes.

2. Cindy uses 9 craft sticks to make the figure as shown.
How many figures can she make with 63 craft sticks?

She can make _____ figures.

3. Ian puts 54 cups into 9 stacks equally.
How many cups are there in each stack?

There are _____ cups in each stack.

4E Multiply by Tens

Paula wants to arrange her stickers into 3 rows of 20. What are the different ways to find the number of stickers she has?

$3 \times 2 = ?$
$3 \times 20 = ?$

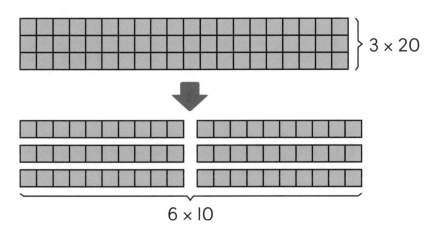

Learn

$$3 \times 20$$

$$6 \times 10$$

$3 \times 20 = 6 \times 10$

3×2 tens $= 6$ tens

= _____

She has _____ stickers.

Learn Together

1. Multiply 20 by 5.

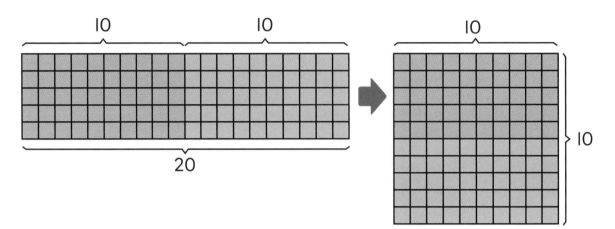

$20 \times 5 = 10 \times$ _____

_____ tens

$=$ _____

2. Multiply 5 by 30.

$5 \times 30 =$ _____ $\times 10$

5×3 tens $=$ _____ tens

$=$ _____

3. Write the missing numbers.

(a) $3 \times 20 =$ _____

(b) $20 \times 5 =$ _____

(c) $6 \times$ _____ $= 240$

$6 \times$ _____ $= 24$

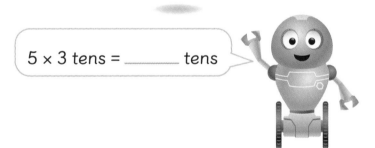

Practice On Your Own 📝

Write the missing numbers.

1. **(a)** $4 \times 30 =$ _____ $\times 10$

    $=$ _____

    (b) $3 \times 40 =$ _____ $\times 10$

    $=$ _____

2. **(a)** $6 \times 30 =$ _____

    (b) $30 \times 8 =$ _____

    (c) _____ $\times 4 = 80$

    (d) _____ $\times 2 = 60$

    (e) $20 \times$ _____ $= 140$

Think!

3. LOOK FOR PATTERNS Complete the table.

a	b	c
2	40	80
7	30	
6		300
	50	250

$a \times b = c$

4. USE STRUCTURE This is a '20 times' machine. Write the missing numbers.

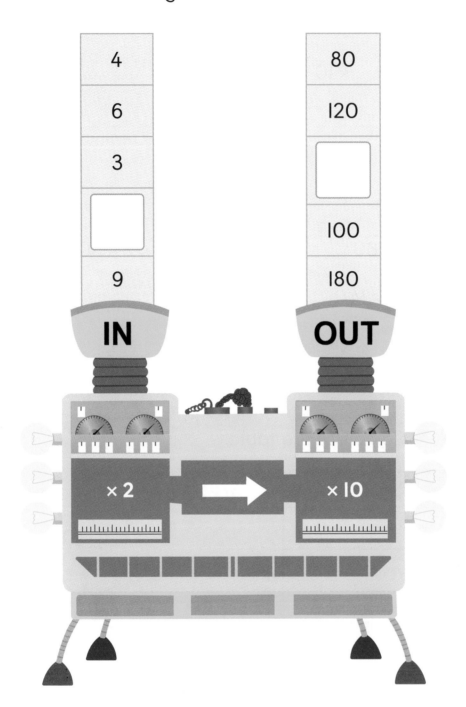

$4 \times 2 \times 10 = 80$

$3 \times 20 = $ _____

_____ $\times 20 = 100$

4F Multiply a 2-Digit Number by a 1-Digit Number

Rita has 3 packs of game cards.
There are 12 game cards in a pack.
What are the different ways
to find the total number
of game cards?

$3 \times 10 = ?$
$3 \times 12 = ?$

Learn

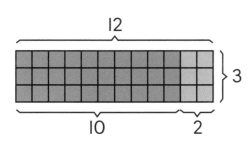

$$12 \times 3 = (10 \times 3) + (2 \times 3)$$
$$= 30 + 6$$
$$= 36$$

```
  T O
  1 2
×   3
─────
    6   Multiply 2 by 3
  3 0   Multiply 10 by 3
─────
  3 6   Add
```

Rita has 36 game cards altogether.

Learn Together

1. Sharon needs 3 ropes of equal length to tie down the sails on her boat. Each rope is 16 inches long.
   What is the total length of rope she uses?

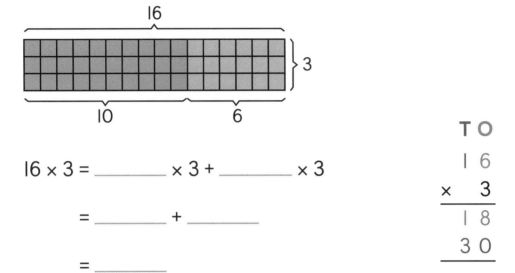

$16 \times 3 =$ _____ $\times 3 +$ _____ $\times 3$

$=$ _____ $+$ _____

$=$ _____

$$
\begin{array}{r}
\text{T O} \\
1\ 6 \\
\times \quad 3 \\
\hline
1\ 8 \\
3\ 0 \\
\hline
\end{array}
$$

The total length of rope is _____ inches.

2. Multiply 19 by 5.

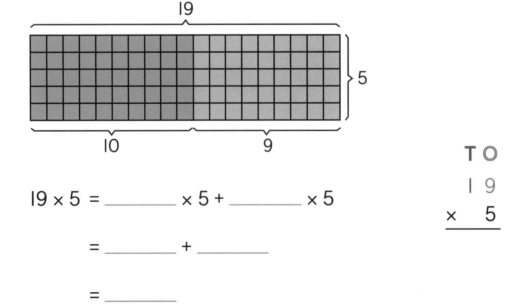

$19 \times 5 =$ _____ $\times 5 +$ _____ $\times 5$

$=$ _____ $+$ _____

$=$ _____

$$
\begin{array}{r}
\text{T O} \\
1\ 9 \\
\times \quad 5 \\
\hline
\end{array}
$$

3. Find the products.

(a) 16 × 5 = _____

$$\begin{array}{r} 1\ 6 \\ \times\quad 5 \\ \hline \end{array}$$

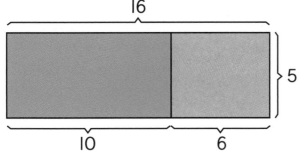

(b) 3 × 25 = _____

$$\begin{array}{r} 2\ 5 \\ \times\quad 3 \\ \hline \end{array}$$

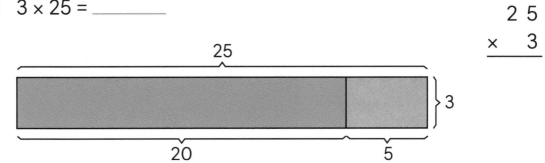

4. **(a)** 43 × 2 = _____   **(b)** 2 × 59 = _____

Practice On Your Own

Find the products.

1. Draw to show your work.

   (a) 21 × 3 = _____

   (b) 18 × 5 = _____

2. **(a)** 2 × 34 = _____   **(b)** 5 × 24 = _____

Name: _____ Date: _____

4G Word Problems

Mrs. Thompson packs 8 backpacks with pens and notebooks for a donation drive. She has 32 pens and some notebooks.

(a) She puts an equal number of pens into each backpack. How many pens are there in each backpack?

(b) She puts 2 notebooks into each backpack. What is the total number of school supplies in each backpack?

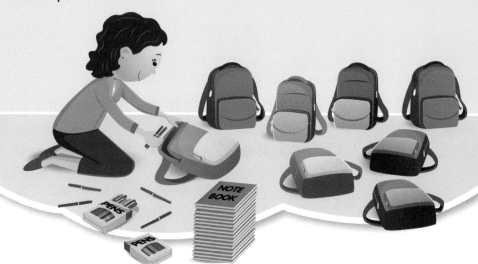

Learn

(a)

What do I know?
What do I have to find?

32

?

$32 \div 8 =$ _____

There are _____ pens in each backpack.

(b)

What do I know now?
What do I have to find?

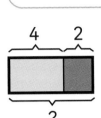

4 + 2 = _____

There are a total of _____ school supplies in each backpack.

Check:

_____ – 2 = 4   (There are 4 pens in each backpack.)

_____ × 8 = 32   (There are 32 pens in all.)

The answers are correct.

Learn Together

1. Alan collects jerseys of his favorite baseball teams.
He keeps 10 baseball jerseys in each of the 9 drawers.
He still has 12 jerseys left.
   (a) How many jerseys are in the drawers?
   (b) How many jerseys are there in all?

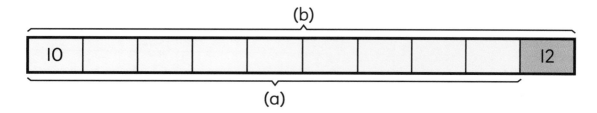

(b)

(a) _____ ◯ _____ = _____

_____ jerseys are in the drawers.

(b) _____ ◯ _____ = _____

There are _____ jerseys in all.

2. Howard saved $319. He used some of his savings to buy a present for his mother and spent the rest on 3 books. Each book cost $23.
   (a) How much did he spend on the books?
   (b) How much did he spend on the present for his mother?

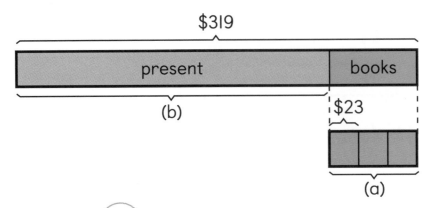

$319

present   books

(b) $23

(a)

(a) _____ ◯ _____ = _____

He spent $_____ on the books.

(b) _____ ◯ _____ = _____

He spent $_____ on the present.

Practice On Your Own 📝

Solve. Show your work.

I. There are 12 third graders. Each of them sells 5 tickets for a school carnival. They sell 16 more tickets than the fourth graders.
   (a) How many tickets do the third graders sell in all?
   (b) How many tickets do the fourth graders sell in all?

   (a)

   The third graders sell _____ tickets in all.

   (b)

   The fourth graders sell _____ tickets in all.

2. At a school assembly, 57 children took part in the drama performance. After the performance, 25 children left the stage. The rest of the children then danced in groups of 4.

    (a) How many children were there in the dance performance?

    (b) How many groups of children were there in the dance performance?

(a)

There were _____ children in the dance performance.

(b)

There were _____ groups of children in the dance performance.

Amy buys 5 boxes of muffins and some bagels.
Each box has 12 muffins.
She buys 33 more muffins than bagels.
How many bagels does Amy buy?

Learn

What do I know?
I draw a bar model to help me understand the problem.

12

muffins

bagels

? 33

What do I have to find first?
What do I need to find next?

Total number of muffins:

$5 \times 12 =$ _____

Number of bagels:

_____ $- 33 =$ _____

Amy buys _____ bagels.

Check:

Total number of muffins:

_____ $+ 33 =$ _____

Number of muffins in a box:

_____ $\div 5 =$ _____

The answer is correct.

Learn Together

I. Mr. Patel buys a desk and 3 chairs. The desk costs $58 and each chair costs $24. How much does Mr. Patel pay for the desk and 3 chairs?

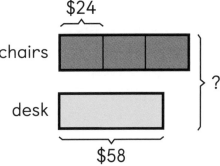

_____ ◯ _____ = _____

The 3 chairs cost $_____.

_____ ◯ _____ = _____

Mr. Patel pays $_____ for the desk and 3 chairs.

2. Ms. Wright earns $200 a week delivering pizza. Each week, she spends $105 and saves the rest. How much does she save at the end of 3 weeks?

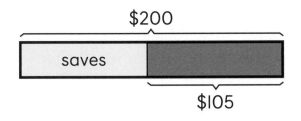

_____ ◯ _____ = _____

She saves $_____ each week.

_____ ◯ _____ = _____

She saves $_____ at the end of 3 weeks.

Practice On Your Own

Solve. Show your work.

1. Cooper packed 15 muffins into boxes of 5 each. He used
    22 inches of tape to seal each box. What is the total length of
    tape he used?

    The total length of tape he used is _____ inches.

2. A Ferris wheel has 9 cabins, each filled with an equal number
    of people. 15 people are still in the line. There are 87 people
    altogether. How many people are there in each cabin?

    There are _____ people in each cabin.

Performance Task

A factory produces fruit pies in three sizes, small, regular, and large. The pies are of the same height.

6 cm

small

7 cm

regular

8 cm

large

The factory manager wants to pack the pies into equal-sized boxes. The base of each box is a square of side length 36 centimeters.

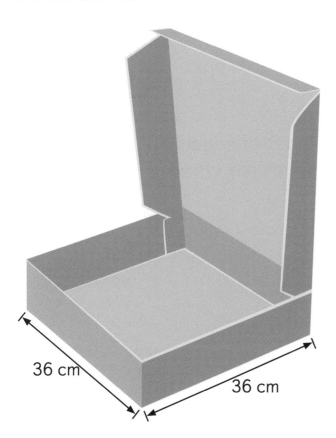

36 cm

36 cm

The pies must be laid neatly in rows and columns.
Each box can pack only one layer of pies.

1. How many small pies can be packed into a box?
Draw to show your work.

_____ small pies can be packed into a box.

2. `REASON` What is the greatest number of regular pies that can be packed into a box? Explain your answer.

The greatest number of regular pies that can be packed

into a box is _____.

3. MODEL What are two possible arrangements to pack different sizes of pies into a box? Draw to show your work.

4. REASON AND MODEL Design a box that can fit exactly 6 large pies. Draw and explain your answer.

How Did I Do?

☺ ☺ ☺	☐ My work is accurate. ☐ I explain my thinking clearly. ☐ I can apply my thinking in word problems. ☐ I can justify why my strategy fits the situation.
☺ ☺	☐ I am mostly accurate. ☐ I explain my thinking clearly. ☐ I can apply my thinking to calculations. ☐ I can use multiple strategies.
☺	☐ I show little work. ☐ I do not explain my thinking clearly. ☐ I am struggling with word problems. ☐ I can only think of one way to solve a problem.

My Teacher's Words

Chapter Practice

1. There are 8 wheels on a truck.
   How many wheels are there on 5 trucks?

Ⓐ 32   Ⓑ 38

Ⓒ 40   Ⓓ 48

2. Write a multiplication equation.

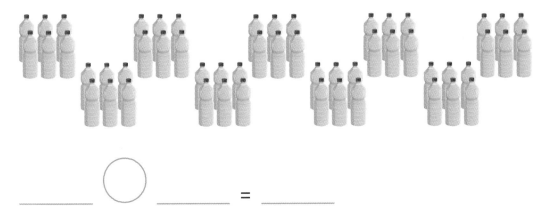

_____ ◯ _____ = _____

3. Write the missing numbers.

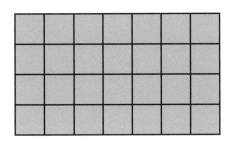

$4 \times \rule{2cm}{0.4pt} = 28$

$28 \div \rule{2cm}{0.4pt} = 4$

4. Write >, =, or <.

(a) 7×8 ◯ 8×8

(b) $72 \div 8$ ◯ $72 \div 9$

(c) 6×5 ◯ $24 + 6$

(d) 9×7 ◯ $54 - 18$

5. Write the missing numbers.

(a) $9 \times$ _____ $+ 9 \times$ _____ $= 9 \times 6$

(b) $8 \times$ _____ $= 4 \times$ _____

6. Multiply a number by 8.
Add 44 to the answer and the sum is 100.
What is the number?

$$\boxed{} \xrightarrow{\times 8} \boxed{} \xrightarrow{+ 44} 100$$

7. Anna packs 72 oranges into 9 bags. Each bag has p oranges. What is the value of p?

The value of p is _____.

8. 10 children go to gym class 3 times a week after school.
Each time they go there, they do 28 jumping jacks each.
(a) How many jumping jacks does a child do in a week?
(b) How many jumping jacks do the children do in all?

(a)

A child does _____ jumping jacks in a week.

(b)

They do _____ jumping jacks in all.

9. A sticker book has 8 sheets. Each sheet has 3 stickers.
How many stickers are there in 3 sticker books?

There are _____ stickers in 3 sticker books.

10. Alexa uses 81 beads to make 9 identical necklaces. She then buys more beads and adds 15 more to each necklace. How many beads are there on each necklace now?

There are _____ beads on each necklace now.

11. PERSEVERE There are 36 desks in a hall. Mr. Johnson wants to arrange the desks into equal rows. How many different arrangements can he make?

He can make _____ different arrangements.

Solve! Heuristics: Guess and Check

Sharon collected drink cans for recycling. She collected a total of 25 cans over 5 days. Each day, she collected 1 more can than the previous day. How many cans did she collect on the first day?

Step 1 **Understand**

> Did Sharon collect the same number of cans each day? How many cans did she collect on the first day?

Step 2 **Plan**

> I decide to make a **guess** and then **check** to see if it works.

Step 3 **Do**

Since 25 ÷ 5 = 5, I can start my first guess using 5.

	Number of cans collected on the first day	Total number of cans collected in 5 days	Check
Guess 1	5	5 + 6 + 7 + 8 + 9 = 35	✗
Guess 2	4	4 + 5 + 6 + 7 + 8 = 30	✗
Guess 3	3	3 + 4 + 5 + 6 + 7 = 25	✓

Sharon collected 3 cans on the first day.

Step 4 **Look Back**
Check that the answer makes sense.

> Is there another way to solve the problem?

Solve.

1. Aki has some five-dollar and some ten-dollar bills. He has 12 bills and $75 in all. How many of each type of bill does he have?

2. Fill the magic triangle with the numbers 1, 2, 3, 4, 5, and 6. The sum of the numbers on each side of the triangle must be 9. The number 2 is given.

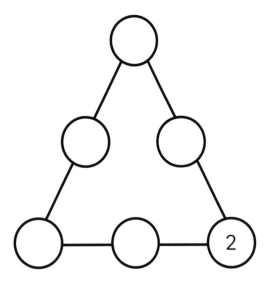

5 TIME

What time is lunch? What time does it end?

How does knowing the time help you in your daily life?

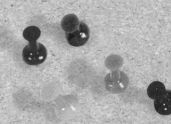

Recall

I.   Write **past** or **to** to tell the time.

(a)

15 minutes _____ 6

(b)

10 minutes _____ 11

2.   Write the time.

(a)

_____ : _____

(b)

_____ : _____

3.   Write the time using **a.m.** or **p.m.**

(a)

It is _____.

(b)

It is _____.

I can...
- ☐ tell time to 5 minutes.
- ☐ use a.m. and p.m. to tell time.

5A Hours and Minutes

Owen goes to school in the morning.
What time does he board the school bus?

Learn

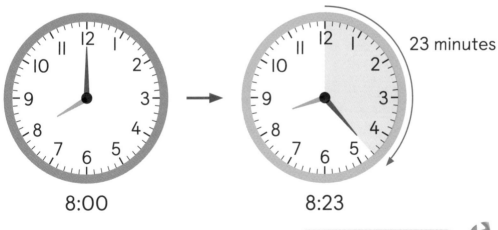

8:00 → 8:23   23 minutes

8:23 is 23 minutes after 8 o'clock.

The time is 23 minutes past 8.
Owen boards the school bus at 8:23 a.m.

Learn Together

Write the time.

1.

? minutes

_____ minutes past _____

_____ : _____

2.

? minutes

_____ minutes to _____

_____ : _____

3. (a)

_____ minutes past 6

_____ : _____

(b)

_____ minutes to 4

_____ : _____

4. Draw the minute hands.

(a) 8 minutes past 5

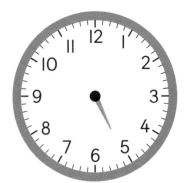

(b) 8 minutes to 5

5. Write the time. You may use to help you.

(a) 13 minutes past 1 is _____.

(b) 9:02 is _____ minutes past _____.

6. Write the time. You may use to help you.

(a) 5 minutes to 7 is _____.

(b) 11:44 is _____ minutes to _____.

Activity!

MODEL Show 6 minutes past 2 and 6 minutes to 2 on and write the time.

Tell your classmate how you count the minutes to find the time.

Practice On Your Own

I. Write the time.

(a)

_____ minutes past _____

_____ : _____

(b)

_____ minutes to _____

_____ : _____

2. Draw the minute hands.

(a) 6 minutes past 4   (b) 17 minutes to 2

3. Write the time.

(a) 15 minutes past 3 is _____.

(b) 7:21 is _____ minutes past _____.

4. Write the time.

(a) 26 minutes to 11 is _____.

(b) 12:56 is _____ minutes to _____.

Jane starts eating breakfast
at 8:15 a.m.
She finishes her food at 8:40 a.m.
How long does she take
to finish her breakfast?

Learn

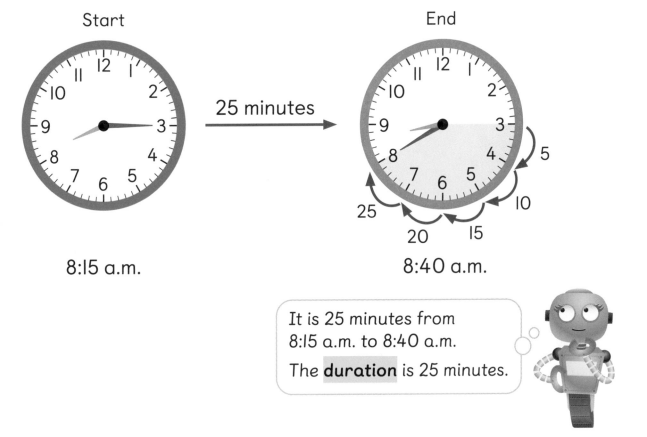

Start

8:15 a.m.

25 minutes →

End

8:40 a.m.

It is 25 minutes from
8:15 a.m. to 8:40 a.m.

The **duration** is 25 minutes.

Jane takes _____ minutes to finish her breakfast.

Learn Together

Write the missing numbers.

1.

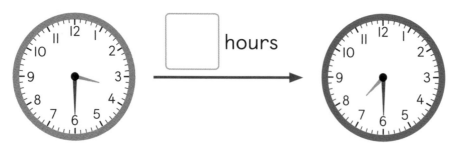

□ hours

2.

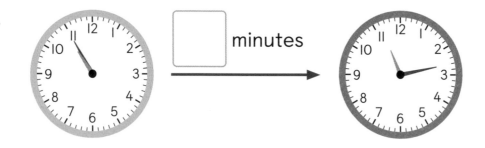

□ minutes

3.

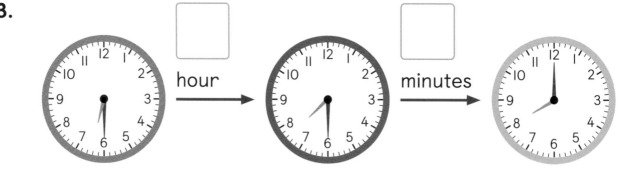

□ hour

□ minutes

1 h 30 min = 60 min + 30 min

1 h = 60 min

= _____ min

The **hour (h)** and **minute (min)** are units of time.

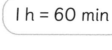

4.

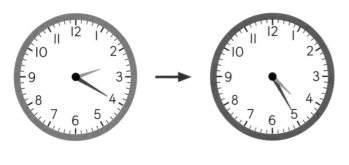

_____ h _____ min

Activity!

MODEL Have your classmate time you as you write as many letters as you can in one minute. If you kept going, how many letters can you write in one hour? Share your answer.

Practice On Your Own

Write the missing numbers.

1.

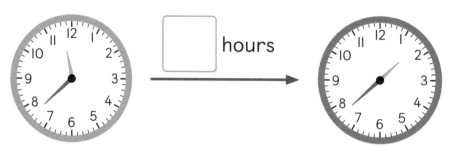

☐ hours

2.

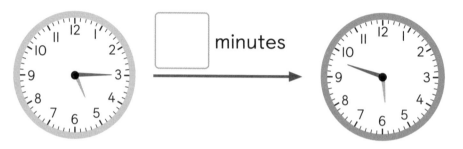

☐ minutes

3.

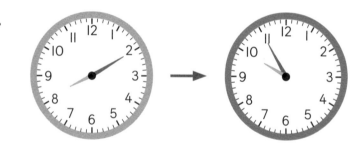

_____ h _____ min = _____ min + _____ min

= _____ min

4.

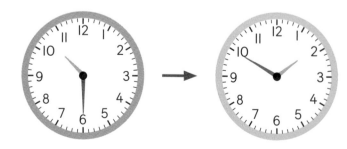

_____ h _____ min

5B Word Problems

A plane departs from Minneapolis at 10:00 a.m. It arrives in New Orleans at 12:46 p.m. How long does the flight take?

MSP — MSY
Fly High Airlines

| 10:00 a.m. | Depart MSP **Minneapolis** |
| 12:46 p.m. | Arrive MSY **New Orleans** |

| Seat | Teminal | Gate |
| 17C | 2 | A6 |

Learn

Step 1 | **Draw a timeline to help you understand the problem.**

What do I know?
What do I have to find?

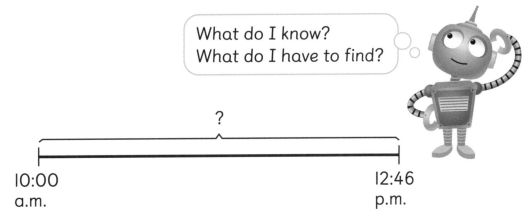

Step 2 | **Solve.**

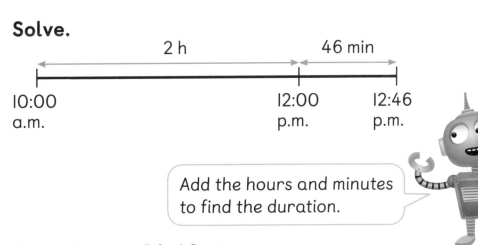

Add the hours and minutes to find the duration.

2 h + 46 min = 2 h 46 min
The flight takes 2 hours 46 minutes.

Check.

12:46 p.m. is around 1:00 p.m.
From 10:00 a.m. to 12:46 p.m., the duration is about 3 hours.
The answer is reasonable.

Learn Together

1. A movie starts at 11:00 a.m. and ends at 12:20 p.m. How long does the movie last?

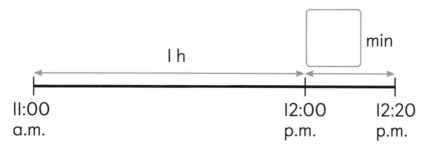

1 h + _____ min = _____ h _____ min

The movie lasts _____ hour _____ minutes.

2. Gabriel takes 30 minutes to do his mathematics homework. He takes 1 hour 5 minutes to do his science project. How much time does he take altogether? Give the answer in hours and minutes.

1 h 5 min + 30 min = _____ h _____ min

He takes _____ hour _____ minutes altogether.

3. Evan takes 65 minutes to complete a jigsaw puzzle. Pablo takes 80 minutes to complete the same jigsaw puzzle. Who takes a longer time? How much longer?

_____ min − _____ min = _____ min

_____ takes _____ minutes longer.

Tell your classmate how long you took to eat breakfast this morning. Who took a longer time?

Practice On Your Own

Solve. Show your work.

1. Audrey and her family went to the beach. They arrived at the beach at 9:15 a.m. They left the beach at 12:00 p.m. How much time did they spend on the beach?

They spent _____ on the beach.

2. It takes 1 hour 15 minutes to prepare the ingredients for a pie. It takes 1 hour 20 minutes to bake the pie. How long does it take in all? Give the answer in hours and minutes.

It takes _____ in all.

3. A plumber takes 45 minutes to fix the kitchen sink. He takes 70 minutes to fix the bathroom sink. Which sink takes a longer time to fix? How much longer?

The _____ sink takes _____ minutes longer to fix.

Think!

4. CONSTRUCT VIABLE ARGUMENTS Liam and Zara are doing laundry. It takes 45 minutes for the washing machine to finish its cycle and 1 hour 10 minutes for the dryer to be done. Liam and Zara are figuring out how long it takes in all to finish the laundry.

Liam's answer

1 h 10 min + 45 min = 1 h 55 min
1 h 55 min = 60 min + 55 min
                    = 115 min

Zara's answer

1 h 10 min + 45 min = 1 h 55 min
1 h 55 min = 100 min + 55 min
                    = 155 min

Who is correct? Explain your answer.

Mrs. Watson goes to the shopping mall.
She leaves her home at 4:45 p.m.
She takes 35 minutes to reach
the mall.
What time does
she reach the mall?

City Mall

Learn

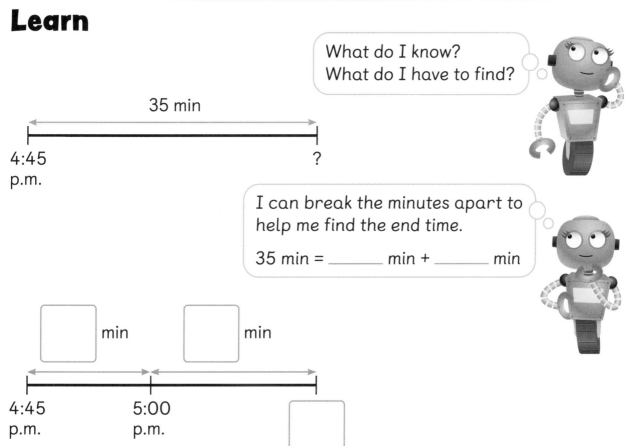

What do I know?
What do I have to find?

35 min

4:45
p.m.   ?

I can break the minutes apart to
help me find the end time.

35 min = _____ min + _____ min

[ ] min   [ ] min

4:45   5:00
p.m.   p.m.   [ ]

She reaches the mall at _____.

Check:
20 minutes before 5:20 p.m. is 5:00 p.m.
15 minutes before 5:00 p.m. is 4:45 p.m.
The answer is correct.

Learn Together

1. Paige reaches the library at 1:20 p.m. She spends 55 minutes at the library. What time does she leave the library?

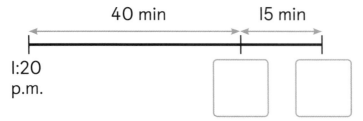

    She leaves the library at _____.

2. Nathan takes a nap for 2 hours 35 minutes. He wakes up at 5:45 p.m. What time does he go to sleep?

    He goes to sleep at _____.

3. Mrs. Lee leaves home at 7:50 a.m. She usually takes 40 minutes to reach her office. Today, she takes 25 minutes longer because of a traffic jam. What time does she reach her office today?

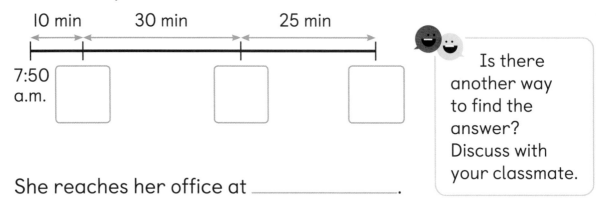

    Is there another way to find the answer? Discuss with your classmate.

    She reaches her office at _____.

Activity!

Use to show 9:00. Take turns spinning the gameboard.

Record the duration you obtained and show the time on .

Practice On Your Own

Solve. Show your work.

I.   A fruit stand opens at 10:30 a.m. It is open for
      6 hours 55 minutes. What time does the stand close?

The stand closes at _____.

2. Ashley spends 1 hour 20 minutes reading a book. She stops reading at 8:25 p.m. What time does she start reading the book?

She starts reading the book at _____.

3. Mr. Walker leaves home at 8:30 a.m. He drives for 25 minutes to a restaurant. He eats breakfast for 30 minutes and then drives another 15 minutes to get to his office. What time does he arrive at his office?

He arrives at his office at _____.

Think!

4. REASON Connor wants to watch the musical fountain show at a theme park. The show runs every 75 minutes starting at 3:00 p.m. He has to leave the theme park at 6:30 p.m. The show lasts 20 minutes. What time is the latest show he can watch? Explain your answer.

Performance Task

The showtimes for some movies at a movie theater are shown below. Some details are missing.

Movie	Return of Dinosaurs	Princess Adventure	Cartoons Galore	Galaxy Adventure
Run time	1 h 15 min	1 h 23 min	?	1 h 42 min
1st show	11:50 a.m.	?	11:30 a.m.	11:45 a.m.
2nd show	1:45 p.m.	2:30 p.m.	2:00 p.m.	2:30 p.m.
3rd show	4:20 p.m.	6:20 p.m.	4:45 p.m.	5:20 p.m.
4th show	8:45 p.m.	8:00 p.m.	7:30 p.m.	8:30 p.m.

1. Cartoons Galore lasts 11 minutes longer than Princess Adventure. How long does Cartoons Galore last? Give the answer in hours and minutes.

    Cartoons Galore lasts _____.

2. The 1st show of Princess Adventure ends at 1:53 p.m. What time does the movie start?

    The movie starts at _____.

3. Blake and his father want to watch a movie. They leave home at 11:20 a.m. and take 30 minutes to reach the movie theater. They arrive just in time for the movie. Which movie do they watch?

They watch the _____ show of _____.

4. REASON Malia and her friends want to watch the 3rd show of Galaxy Adventure. They have to leave the movie theater at 6:30 p.m. Should they watch the movie? Explain your answer.

5. Mr. and Mrs. Baker want to take their child to watch a movie.
The tickets cost $9 for each adult and $8 for each child.
How much do they have to pay for the movie tickets?

They have to pay $_____ for the movie tickets.

6. MODEL Plan the showtimes for another movie. The movie
theater is open from 11:30 a.m. to 10:30 p.m. There are
four shows for a movie each day.

Movie	
Run time	
1st show	
2nd show	
3rd show	
4th show	

How Did I Do?

☐ My work is accurate.
☐ I explain my thinking clearly.
☐ I can apply my thinking in word problems.
☐ I can justify why my strategy fits the situation.

☐ I am mostly accurate.
☐ I explain my thinking clearly.
☐ I can apply my thinking to calculations.
☐ I can use multiple strategies.

☐ I show little work.
☐ I do not explain my thinking clearly.
☐ I am struggling with word problems.
☐ I can only think of one way to solve a problem.

My Teacher's Words

Chapter Practice

I.   Write the time.

(a)

_____ : _____

(b)

_____ : _____

2.   Draw the minute hands.

(a) 4:17 p.m.

(b) 1:52 a.m.

3.   Write the time.

(a) 6:11 is _____ minutes past _____.

(b) 3:48 is _____ minutes to _____.

4. How long is it from 11:20 p.m. to 2:43 a.m.?

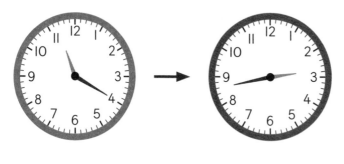

_____ h _____ min

5. Mr. Nelson takes 18 minutes to drive from his home to the mall. He takes 24 minutes to drive from the mall to his friend's home. How long does he drive in all?

(A) 42 minutes   (B) 35 minutes

(C) 6 minutes   (D) 10 minutes

6. A storytime session at the library lasts 25 minutes. It ends at 3:10 p.m. What time does it start?

(A) 2:45 a.m.   (B) 2:45 p.m.

(C) 3:35 a.m.   (D) 3:35 p.m.

7. Mr. Torres starts mowing his lawn at 11:45 a.m. He stops mowing at 12:20 p.m. How long does he take to mow his lawn?

He takes _____ minutes to mow his lawn.

8. An athlete trains for 75 minutes on Monday. He trains for 110 minutes on Tuesday. On which day does he train for a longer time? How much longer?

He trains for _____ minutes longer on _____.

9. A Broadway musical starts at 5:30 p.m. and lasts 1 hour 33 minutes. What time does the musical end?

The musical ends at _____.

10. Mr. Gomez finishes cooking lunch at 12:35 p.m. He takes 1 hour 25 minutes to cook lunch. What time does he start cooking lunch?

He starts cooking lunch at _____.

II. REASON An antique clock on a wall is 15 minutes slow. If the clock shows 9:55 p.m., what is the actual time? Explain your answer.

12. PERSEVERE Jessica is folding paper cranes. She can fold 10 paper cranes in 15 minutes. She takes 5 minutes of rest for every 15 minutes of folding. How long will she take to fold 40 paper cranes?

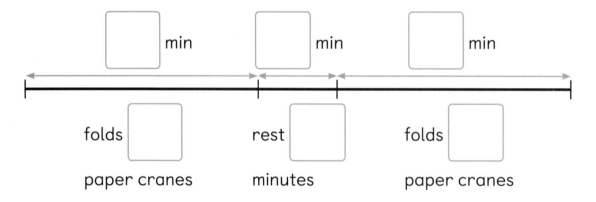

Glossary

array

An array shows the rows and columns of objects.

The array shows 3 rows of 5.

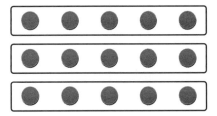

The array shows 5 columns of 3.

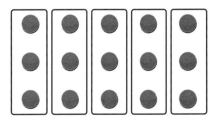

D

divide

You divide to find the number in each group.

$6 \div 3 = 2$
There are 2 sandwiches in each group.

You also divide to find the number of equal groups.
$6 \div 2 = 3$
There are 3 equal groups of sandwiches.

division equation

$6 \div 3 = 2$ is a division equation.

duration

Duration is the amount of time that has passed between the start time and the end time of an activity.

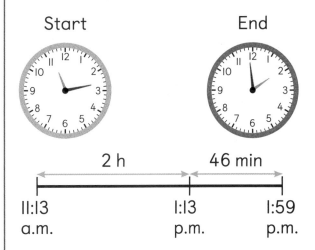

The duration is 2 hours 46 minutes.

estimate

An estimate is a number that is close to the actual number.

480 is about 500 when rounded to the nearest hundred.

2,129 is about 2,100 when rounded to the nearest hundred.

An estimated sum of 480 and 2,129 is 500 + 2,100 = 2,600.

hour (h)

The hour (h) is a unit of time.
1 hour = 60 minutes

See **minute**.

minute (min)

The minute (min) is a unit of time.
60 minutes = 1 hour

See **hour**.

multiply

You multiply to find the total when you put together equal groups.

There are 3 groups. There are 2 erasers in each group.
3 × 2 = 6
There are 6 erasers in all.

multiplication equation

3 × 2 = 6 is a multiplication equation.

product

When you multiply two numbers, you get the product.

12 × 3 = 36
The product of 12 and 3 is 36.

Q

quotient

When you divide one number by another, you get the quotient.

$24 \div 6 = 4$
When 24 is divided by 6, the quotient is 4.

R

round

When you round a number, you estimate the number to the nearest ten or nearest hundred.

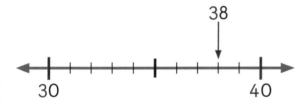

38 rounded to the nearest ten is 40.

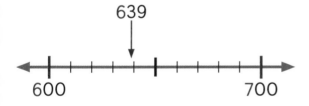

639 rounded to the nearest hundred is 600.

T

ten thousand

Ten thousand is one more than nine thousand, nine hundred ninety-nine.

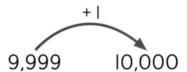

Index

Photo Credits

BLANK